Market Microstructure

The Hidden Mechanics of Trading

William Johnson

Published by HiTeX Press

For permissions and other inquiries, write to:
P.O. Box 3132, Framingham, MA 01701, USA

Contents

Preface

Imagine standing at the edge of a bustling marketplace, a place where fortunes are made and lost in the blink of an eye. The clamor of traders fills the air, each vying for a piece of the action, each guided by their strategies, motivations, and instincts. This marketplace is the stock market, a dynamic arena where financial instruments are traded, prices are discovered, and the pulse of the economy can be felt. But, beneath this frenetic surface lies a world of hidden mechanics and intricate structures. Welcome to the realm of market microstructure.

This book, "Market Microstructure: The Hidden Mechanics of Trading," ventures into the very heart of the financial markets. It reveals the sophisticated underpinnings behind every trade, the nuanced dance of buyers and sellers, the roles of various participants, and the technologies that have revolutionized trading. Through this exploration, we unveil the core message of the book: an understanding of market microstructure is pivotal for anyone who seeks to navigate the complex world of financial markets successfully.

From the different types of orders and the workings of order books to the processes that drive price discovery and liquidity, this book covers it all. We delve into the roles of market makers, the enigmatic realm of high-frequency trading, and the impacts of regulation and market design. We also explore the critical aspects of risk management, the ever-evolving landscape of algorithmic strategies, and future directions in market microstructure, such as the influence of blockchain and artificial intelligence.

Once you grasp these concepts, you will see the markets through a new lens. You'll understand how trades are executed, why certain events trigger price movements, and how market participants interact within the microstructure to create the larger market picture. Knowledge is power, and by equipping yourself with this understanding, you will gain a significant edge in your trading and investment endeavors.

The benefits of mastering market microstructure are manifold. By comprehending the inner workings of the stock market, you can make informed decisions, mitigate risks more effectively, and refine your trading strategies to align with the underlying market mechanics. Whether you are a novice investor, a seasoned trader, or a finance professional, this book provides valuable insights that enhance your financial acumen and operational success.

As we embark on this journey through the hidden mechanics of trading, let this book be your guide and companion. There is much to discover, much to learn, and much to apply. The world of market microstructure is intricate and fascinating, and its principles are crucial to understanding the financial markets' true nature.

So, turn the page, dive into the depths, and unlock the secrets of market microstructure. The insights you gain will transform the way you view and interact with the financial markets, empowering you to achieve your trading and investment goals with confidence and clarity. Let's begin this compelling exploration together.

Chapter 1

Introduction to Market Microstructure

Market microstructure examines the intricate mechanisms and structures underpinning financial markets, focusing on the processes through which securities are traded and priced. This chapter delves into the foundational concepts and historical evolution of market microstructure, elucidates key terminology, and highlights its significant role in shaping market behavior and efficiency. It also identifies the various participants in financial markets and provides an overview of the diverse trading mechanisms in place today, emphasizing the critical impact of technology in modern trading environments.

1.1   Understanding Market Microstructure

Market microstructure is a fascinating field that provides a deep dive into the mechanics of how markets operate at the granular level. It transcends the superficial understanding of market movements and digs into the intricate details of trading processes, price formation, and the behavior of different market participants. This section aims to demystify these concepts, providing a comprehensive understanding suitable for both newcomers and seasoned market professionals.

At its core, market microstructure focuses on the mechanisms that facilitate the exchange of securities and the determination of their prices. These mechanisms involve a complex interplay of various factors including order types, execution processes, market liquidity, and the role of information. To appreciate the full scope of market microstructure, consider the analogy of a watch's internal mechanics. While the face of the watch displays the time, it is the intimate workings of its gears and springs that make it function correctly. Similarly, while we observe stock prices and trade volumes, it is the underlying market microstructure that defines how these prices are set and how trades are executed.

One of the foundational elements of market microstructure is the concept of an *order book*. The order book is a dynamic record containing all buy and sell orders for a particular security at various price levels. Market participants place orders, either to buy (bid) or sell (ask), and these orders populate the order book. The highest price a buyer is willing to pay for a security and the lowest price a seller is willing to accept intersect to form the market price. This matching process, influenced by the supply and demand dynamics embodied within the order book, is central to price discovery.

It is essential to differentiate between two primary types of orders: *market orders* and *limit orders*. A market order is an instruction to buy or sell immediately at the best available price, guaranteeing execution but not the price. Conversely, a limit order specifies the price at which a participant is willing to buy or sell, providing control over the execution price but not guaranteeing an immediate transaction. The interplay of these orders within the order book significantly affects market liquidity and the speed of price adjustments.

An advanced concept within market microstructure is *market depth*. Market depth refers to the quantity of buy and sell orders at various price levels away from the current market price. High market depth indicates a large number of orders close to the current price, suggesting greater liquidity and the ability to absorb larger trades without significantly impacting prices. Conversely, shallow market depth can lead to higher price volatility and execution costs.

The behavior of different market participants also shapes market microstructure. Participants range from individual retail investors to large institutional traders, high-frequency traders (HFTs), and market makers. Each group interacts with the market differently based on their strategies and objectives. Market makers, for instance, are crucial for providing liquidity by continuously posting buy and sell orders, thus narrowing bid-ask spreads and enhancing market efficiency. High-frequency traders, leveraging advanced algorithms and technology, seek to profit from tiny price discrepancies, contributing to increased trading volume and market fluidity.

Information asymmetry is another critical component. In a perfectly symmetric information environment, all participants would have equal access to market-moving information, facilitating fair and efficient price discovery. However, in reality, some participants might have access to superior information, gaining a potential edge. This asymmetry can influence trading behavior and lead to phenomena such as adverse selection, where market makers adjust their quotes to mitigate the risk of trading with better-informed participants. The bid-ask spread often reflects this risk, widening in periods of significant information dispersion.

Furthermore, the role of trading venues in shaping market microstructure cannot be overstated. Markets function through various trading platforms, including traditional exchanges, electronic communication networks (ECNs), and dark pools. Each venue has distinct characteristics and rules that influence the trading process. For instance, traditional exchanges offer transparency and liquidity, while dark pools allow for large trades to be executed with reduced market impact, shielding participants from information leakage.

By understanding market microstructure, investors and traders can better navigate the complexities of trading environments, optimize their strategies, and achieve more favorable outcomes. This knowledge empowers participants to make informed decisions about order placement, execution methods, and the selection of trading venues, ultimately enhancing their ability to manage risk and capitalize on market opportunities.

In essence, market microstructure reveals the underlying mechanisms that drive market behavior, offering a detailed view that goes far beyond price charts and trading volumes. By appreciating these underlying processes, one gains a deeper understanding of how markets function and the factors that influence trading dynamics. This foundational knowledge sets the stage for exploring more advanced topics and strategies in subsequent chapters.

1.2 Historical Development of Market Microstructure

The historical evolution of market microstructure is a tale of continuous adaptation and enhancement to ensure efficiency, transparency, and fairness in financial markets. To comprehend the present complexities of market microstructure, it is essential to trace its development through various pivotal stages.

Early Markets and the Birth of Exchange Trading: The concept of market microstructure finds its roots in the primitive exchanges where physical marketplaces facilitated the trading of goods and securities. One of the earliest recorded exchanges was the Amsterdam Stock Exchange, established in 1602 by the Dutch East India Company. This exchange laid the groundwork for modern stock markets by introducing structured trading environments where buyers and sellers could interact. Orders were placed manually, and the execution of trades relied heavily on direct negotiation, a far cry from the algorithm-fueled trades of today.

The Nineteenth Century: Rise of Organized Exchanges and Market Regulation: The 19th century witnessed the formalization of organized exchanges, significantly transforming the market's microstructure. The New York Stock Exchange (NYSE), founded in 1792, exemplified these changes. The Buttonwood Agreement, signed by 24 stockbrokers under a buttonwood tree, initiated a commission-based system for trading securities, which evolved into a well-defined auction market. Over time, as the volume and complexity of trades increased, these exchanges implemented rules and regulations to regulate conduct, minimize fraud, and stabilize markets. The establishment of the Securities and Exchange Commission (SEC) in 1934 marked a significant milestone in the regulatory landscape, enforcing rules to protect investors and uphold market integrity.

Introduction of Electronic Trading: The latter half of the 20th century introduced transformative technological advancements that reshaped market microstructure. The advent of computers in the 1970s revolutionized trading procedures, particularly with the introduction of the NASDAQ stock market in 1971, which was the first electronic exchange. NASDAQ's use of a computer-based system for matching buy and sell orders signaled the beginning of the shift away from traditional open outcry systems toward electronic trading. This transition facilitated greater accessibility, reduced transaction costs, and enhanced the speed of execution, paving the way for the rise of algorithmic trading and further innovations.

The Impact of Algorithmic and High-Frequency Trading: The 21st century brought with it an extraordinary increase in the complexity of market microstructure, largely driven by the advent of algorithmic and high-frequency trading (HFT). Algorithms—pre-programmed instructions for trading—enabled the rapid execution of complicated trading strategies that respond to market data in real time. High-frequency traders exploit ultra-low latency environments to execute trades within microseconds, capitalizing on minute price discrepancies and contributing significantly to market liquidity. However, the rise of HFT has also introduced challenges, such as increased market volatility and the potential for flash crashes, necessitating sophisticated risk management and regulatory oversight.

Globalization and Market Integration: In parallel, the globalization of financial markets has profoundly impacted market microstructure. Cross-border trading and international exchanges have increased market interconnectedness, reducing geographical barriers and diversifying investment opportunities. This evolution demands robust infrastructure to handle diverse trading regulations and market practices, further complicating the market microstructure.

Modern Developments and Future Directions: Today, markets continuously evolve, driven by artificial intelligence, blockchain technology, and regulatory responses to ever-changing dynamics. Dark pools and alternative trading systems (ATS) have emerged, providing avenues for executing large trades anonymously to mitigate market impact. At the same time, regulators globally strive to balance Innovation with the need for transparency and stability.

Understanding the historical context of market microstructure illuminates how past innovations and regulatory responses have shaped the mechanisms through which today's financial markets operate. As technology and market behaviors continue to evolve, grasping this historical development is invaluable for navigating current and future challenges in trading.

1.3   Key Concepts and Terminology

Understanding the intricacies of market microstructure necessitates a firm grasp of several key concepts and terminology. These foundational elements provide the framework for analyzing and interpreting the dynamics of financial markets, facilitating a deeper comprehension of how markets operate. This section delves into essential terms and concepts, meticulously clarifying their meanings and relevance within the context of market microstructure.

Market microstructure revolves around the mechanisms through which securities are traded, and it is imperative to understand the nature of these mechanisms. The primary notion here is the market itself - a venue where buyers and sellers come together to transact. These can be physical locations like the New York Stock Exchange (NYSE) or virtual platforms like NASDAQ. These markets can function through various trading mechanisms, each carrying distinct features that influence market behavior.

To begin with, **bid** and **ask** prices are fundamental. The *bid price* is the highest price a buyer is willing to pay for a security, while the *ask price* is the lowest price a seller is willing to accept. The difference between these two prices is known as the **bid-ask spread**, a critical concept influencing liquidity and trading costs. A narrower spread typically indicates a more liquid market, whereas a wider spread suggests higher transaction costs and potentially less trading activity.

Next, we consider **order types**, which specify the way traders initiate transactions. The most basic types are **market orders** and **limit orders**. A *market order* is executed immediately at the current market price, emphasizing speed over price certainty. Conversely, a *limit order* is only executed at a specified price or better, prioritizing price precision over execution speed. These order types underpin the strategies traders deploy to achieve their objectives.

The **order book** is the ledger that records all outstanding limit orders, providing a transparent view of the buy and sell sides of the market. This book is continuously updated and is paramount in understanding market depth – a measure of the number of shares that can be traded at the best bid and ask prices. Market depth influences price stability, with greater depth typically leading to lower price volatility.

Another pivotal concept is **market liquidity**, which refers to the ease with which an asset can be bought or sold without causing a significant impact on its price. High liquidity suggests active, frequent trading with minimal price changes, whereas low liquidity implies that trades might significantly affect prices. Liquidity is essential for efficient market functioning, influencing both transaction costs and market stability.

Price discovery is the process through which the market determines the price of a security. It is largely driven by the interactions between buyers and sellers, informed by the order flow and prevailing market conditions. Efficient price discovery ensures that the price of a security reflects all available information, which is crucial for transparent and fair trading environments.

Equally important is the concept of **market efficiency**. This reflects the degree to which asset prices fully incorporate all available information. In an efficient market, securities' prices at any given time are considered to reflect their true value based on all known data. Market efficiency can be categorized into three forms: weak, semi-strong, and strong, each reflecting the extent and type of information that prices are believed to integrate.

A deeper understanding of these concepts provides the necessary foundation for analyzing market microstructure. By mastering these key terms, traders and investors can better interpret market movements and make more informed decisions. As we progress through this book, these foundational elements will continue to play a critical role, elucidating how the hidden mechanics of trading impact overall market behavior.

These core principles - bid-ask spread, order types, order book, market liquidity, price discovery, and market efficiency - are crucial to navigating and comprehending the complex landscape of modern financial markets. As we delve further into the topic, it will become evident how these underlying concepts interact and influence the broader market ecosystem. Keeping these definitions and their implications in mind will enable a more nuanced appreciation of the precise mechanisms that drive market dynamics.

1.4 Importance of Market Microstructure

Understanding market microstructure is pivotal for any trader or investor aiming to navigate the complex landscapes of financial markets adeptly. At its core, market microstructure investigates the processes and systems that facilitate trading in securities such as stocks, bonds, and derivatives. This examination provides insights into various aspects including transaction costs, price discovery, liquidity, and market efficiency. By grasping these concepts, investors gain a significant edge in both strategy formulation and execution.

The price discovery process is a fundamental element in the study of market microstructure. Price discovery refers to the mechanism by which the market determines the price of an asset based on supply and demand dynamics. A well-functioning market microstructure ensures that prices reflect all available information efficiently. This efficiency is crucial for investors, as it allows for the accurate valuation of securities and, consequently, more informed investment decisions.

Additionally, market microstructure directly impacts transaction costs, which can erode investment returns. These costs encompass more than just explicit fees such as brokerage commissions. Implicit costs, including bid-ask spreads and market impact costs, are also significant. The bid-ask spread represents the difference between the price at which a security can be bought and sold at a given point in time. Market impact costs occur when large orders move the market price unfavorably as they are executed. A deep understanding of market microstructure enables investors to strategize around these costs, minimizing their negative effects and optimizing trade execution.

Liquidity, or the ease with which securities can be bought or sold in the market without affecting their price, is another critical aspect of market microstructure. Measures of liquidity often include trading volume and the bid-ask spread. Highly liquid markets allow for quick transactions with minimal price fluctuations. Conversely, illiquid markets are characterized by higher costs of trading and greater price volatility. Knowledge of market microstructure helps investors gauge the liquidity of different assets and adjust their strategies accordingly. For instance, in highly illiquid markets, investors might use limit orders instead of market orders to control execution prices better.

Market efficiency is the capacity of a market to incorporate and reflect all relevant information in the price of securities. Traditional financial theories such as the Efficient Market Hypothesis (EMH) suggest that in an efficient market, it is impossible to achieve consistently higher returns without assuming additional risk. However, various market microstructure elements illustrate that markets might not always be perfectly efficient. Information asymmetry, where some market participants have access to information not available to others, and other frictions can lead to mispricings. Understanding these nuances allows traders to identify and exploit inefficiencies, thereby enhancing their investment performance.

The importance of market microstructure also extends to its role in regulatory frameworks. Regulators scrutinize market structures to ensure fairness, transparency, and protection for all market participants. For example, rules governing order handling and execution aim to prevent manipulative practices and promote a level playing field. Familiarity with these regulations and how they shape trading practices can help investors avoid regulatory pitfalls and leverage opportunities within the legal framework.

Moreover, technological advancements have revolutionized market microstructure, reshaping how participants interact with markets. High-frequency trading (HFT), algorithmic trading, and other sophisticated strategies have emerged, driven by technology. These advancements have dramatically increased the speed and efficiency of markets but also introduced new risks. For instance, flash crashes and other market disruptions are partly attributable to the complexity and speed of modern trading algorithms. An in-depth understanding of the interplay between technology and market microstructure empowers traders to develop robust strategies that mitigate these risks while capitalizing on the technological advantages.

In conclusion, the study of market microstructure equips traders and investors with the knowledge to enhance their market engagement fundamentally. By appreciating how prices are discovered, transaction costs incurred, liquidity evaluated, and efficiency assessed, investors can make more informed decisions. The interplay of these dynamics against the backdrop of regulatory and technological landscapes underscores the complexity and significance of market microstructure in shaping successful trading and investing strategies.

1.5 Participants in Financial Markets

Participants in financial markets play crucial roles that collectively drive the dynamics of trading, pricing, and overall market behavior. Understanding who these participants are, their motivations, and their impact on the markets is fundamental for anyone delving into market microstructure. Here, we explore the primary market participants, categorized by their function and influence in financial markets.

- **Retail Investors:** Retail investors are individual market participants who buy and sell securities for personal accounts, typically in smaller quantities than institutional investors. They are driven by personal financial goals, such as retirement savings, capital growth, or speculation. Despite the relatively smaller volume of their trades, the collective activity of retail investors can significantly influence market trends and liquidity. Retail investors often rely on online brokerage platforms, which have democratized access to financial markets by lowering transaction costs and providing a wealth of educational resources and trading tools.

- **Institutional Investors:** Institutional investors include entities such as pension funds, insurance companies, mutual funds, hedge funds, and sovereign wealth funds. These participants manage large sums of money on behalf of others and engage in trading in substantial volumes. Due to their size and resources, institutional investors exert a considerable impact on market liquidity and price discovery. Their strategies often involve sophisticated analysis and longer investment horizons compared to retail investors. Additionally, the sheer volume of trades executed by institutional investors can lead to more efficient markets, contributing to price stability and reduced volatility.

- **Market Makers:** Market makers are key players in the financial ecosystem, providing liquidity by standing ready to buy and sell securities at publicly quoted prices. Their primary function is to facilitate smoother trading by narrowing the bid-ask spread and ensuring that buyers and sellers can transact with minimal delay. Market makers earn profits from the spread between the buying and selling prices and may also benefit from high trading volumes. By supplying continuous liquidity, market makers help stabilize markets and play a pivotal role in maintaining orderly trading conditions.

- **Brokers and Dealers:** Brokers act as intermediaries between buyers and sellers, executing orders on behalf of their clients for a commission fee. They do not typically hold significant inventory of securities but instead focus on matching buy and sell orders. Dealers, on the other hand, trade for their own accounts, taking on positions in various securities and profiting from market movements. Some firms operate as both brokers and dealers, commonly referred to as broker-dealers. Their dual role allows them to provide comprehensive services to clients while also engaging actively in the markets.

- **Arbitrageurs:** Arbitrageurs seek to exploit price inefficiencies across different markets or financial instruments. They typically engage in buying and selling related securities simultaneously to lock in risk-free profits, correcting mispricings and contributing to market efficiency in the process. For instance, if a stock is priced differently on two exchanges, an arbitrageur will buy it on the cheaper exchange and sell it on the more expensive one, pocketing the differential. While sophisticated and often algorithm-based, arbitrage activities ensure that markets remain aligned and consistent.

- **High-Frequency Traders (HFTs):** High-frequency trading firms utilize advanced algorithms and powerful computing systems to execute a large number of orders at extremely high speeds. These traders typically hold positions for very short durations, sometimes mere milliseconds, profiting from minute price movements. HFTs play a significant role in adding liquidity and narrowing spreads, but their activities have also raised concerns about market stability and fairness, particularly during periods of extreme volatility. Regulatory bodies closely monitor HFT practices to mitigate potential risks to market integrity.

- **Hedge Funds:** Hedge funds are pooled investment vehicles that employ a variety of strategies to achieve high returns for their investors. These strategies may include leveraging, derivatives, short selling, and arbitrage. Hedge funds often operate with fewer regulatory constraints compared to mutual funds, allowing them greater flexibility in their trading tactics. The capital managed by hedge funds can have substantial implications for market liquidity and pricing dynamics, as their trades often involve significant volumes and sophisticated strategies.

- **Algorithmic Traders:** Algorithmic trading involves using computer algorithms to automate trading decisions based on predefined criteria. These algorithms analyze market data in real-time to identify trading opportunities, execute orders, and manage risk. Algorithmic traders range from retail investors using basic strategies to large institutions deploying complex, high-frequency trading systems. Algorithmic trading enhances market efficiency and liquidity but also necessitates robust risk management and regulatory oversight to prevent systemic issues.

- **Regulators and Exchanges:** Regulatory bodies and exchanges form the backbone of financial markets, ensuring a fair, transparent, and smoothly functioning trading environment. Regulators enforce laws and guidelines designed to protect investors, maintain fair trading practices, and promote market integrity. Exchanges provide the platforms where securities are bought and sold, offering transparency, liquidity, and a mechanism for price discovery. Together, regulators and exchanges play a critical role in sustaining market confidence and stability.

Each of these participant groups brings distinct motivations, strategies, and impacts to the financial markets. Their interactions create a dynamic ecosystem where liquidity, pricing efficiency, and market stability evolve continually. For traders and investors, understanding these participants and their interrelationships is vital for navigating the complexities of financial markets and capitalizing on emerging opportunities.

1.6   Overview of Trading Mechanisms

At the core of financial markets lies the varied and sophisticated mechanisms through which trading occurs. These mechanisms determine how orders are matched, prices are established, and trades are executed. A comprehensive understanding of trading mechanisms is essential for both novice and experienced traders, as it illuminates the landscape in which they operate and provides insights into optimizing trading strategies. This section will explore the principal trading mechanisms, including auction markets, dealer markets, order-driven markets, and hybrid markets, each with distinct attributes and implications for market participants.

The auction market represents a traditional but enduring model, with the New York Stock Exchange (NYSE) serving as a preeminent example. In this setting, buyers and sellers congregate, either physically or electronically, to propose their bids and offers. Prices are determined through a process where the highest bid and lowest offer converge, establishing a market-clearing price. There are two primary types of auction markets: continuous and periodic. In a continuous auction market, trading occurs throughout the trading day, with prices frequently updated to reflect new information and orders. Conversely, a periodic auction market consolidates orders and matches them at specific times, often opening and closing sessions. The primary advantages of auction markets include price transparency and competitive pricing, yet they may be limited by lower liquidity and higher volatility during periods of sparse trading activity.

Dealer markets, exemplified by the NASDAQ, operate through intermediaries known as dealers or market makers. These entities provide liquidity by standing ready to buy and sell securities from their own inventory at quoted bid and ask prices. Unlike auction markets, where buyers and sellers interact directly, dealer markets rely on the dealer's active participation. Market makers profit from the spread between their bid and ask prices, absorbing the risk of holding inventory. Dealer markets are particularly effective for less liquid securities, as the continuous participation of dealers supports steady price discovery and trade execution. However, the reliance on dealers introduces concerns about potential conflicts of interest and the fairness of spreads, highlighting the importance of regulatory oversight.

Order-driven markets function distinctively by matching buyer and seller orders directly, eschewing intermediaries. This mechanism is prevalent in electronic communication networks (ECNs) and many modern exchanges outside the United States. The core feature of order-driven markets is the order book, an electronic ledger displaying all outstanding buy and sell orders arranged by price level. Market participants can view order book depth and submit market orders to execute immediately or limit orders to await execution at a specified price. The transparency of order-driven markets facilitates robust price discovery and reduces the execution costs of spreads. However, they may occasionally suffer from liquidity issues, particularly for less actively traded securities.

Hybrid markets, incorporating elements from both auction and dealer markets, leverage the strengths of each to enhance trading efficiency. The NYSE is a prominent example, having evolved its structure to integrate electronic trading systems with traditional floor operations. In hybrid markets, automated trading platforms handle a significant proportion of order flow, ensuring speed and efficiency, while human market makers intervene in periods of high volatility or complexity. This dual approach aims to optimize liquidity, price discovery, and trade execution quality.

In contemporary financial markets, technology plays an indispensable role in the evolution and integration of trading mechanisms. High-frequency trading (HFT), for instance, reflects the convergence of order-driven and dealer market attributes, employing complex algorithms to execute trades at microsecond intervals. HFT leverages the prevalent electronic trading infrastructure to capitalize on minimal price discrepancies and arbitrage opportunities, significantly influencing market dynamics and liquidity profiles.

A comprehensive understanding of these trading mechanisms equips market participants to navigate the evolving landscape of financial markets adeptly. By appreciating the nuances of auction, dealer, order-driven, and hybrid markets, traders can devise informed strategies tailored to the specific mechanics of each system, ultimately enhancing their trading efficiency and effectiveness.

1.7 The Role of Technology in Modern Markets

Technology has revolutionized the landscape of financial markets, transforming the ways in which transactions are executed, analyzed, and monitored. The evolution of market microstructure is inherently tied to advancements in technology, which have facilitated significant improvements in market efficiency, transparency, and accessibility. This section explores the pivotal role that technology plays in modern markets, examining both its immediate impact and its broader implications for the future of trading.

At the heart of this technological transformation is the advent of electronic trading platforms. These platforms have replaced the traditional open outcry systems, enabling traders to execute orders with unprecedented speed and accuracy. By leveraging sophisticated algorithms and advanced computing power, electronic trading platforms minimize the latency between order initiation and execution, thereby reducing the potential for slippage and improving the overall execution quality. For instance, the use of limit order books, which electronically record buy and sell orders, has streamlined the matching process, ensuring that trades are executed at the best possible prices.

$$\text{Execution Quality} = \frac{\text{Number of Optimal Trades}}{\text{Total Number of Trades}}$$

Furthermore, technology has democratized access to financial markets. Online brokerage services and trading applications have lowered the barriers to entry, allowing retail investors to participate alongside institutional players. These platforms provide real-time market data, analytical tools, and educational resources, empowering individual investors to make informed decisions. The integration of mobile technology has further enhanced accessibility, enabling traders to monitor and execute trades on-the-go.

Algorithmic trading, a direct consequence of technological advancement, has emerged as a dominant force in modern markets. Algorithms, or computer-generated instructions, are used to automate trading strategies, ranging from simple rules based on technical indicators to complex models incorporating machine learning. The ability to process vast amounts of data in real-time allows algorithmic traders to identify and capitalize on market inefficiencies. High-frequency trading (HFT), a subset of algorithmic trading, operates on extremely short time frames, executing thousands of trades in milliseconds to profit from minor price movements.

```
def simple_moving_average(data, window):
    return data.rolling(window=window).mean()

prices = get_price_data('AAPL')
sma = simple_moving_average(prices, 20)
```

$$\text{Profit} = (\text{Sell Price} - \text{Buy Price}) \times \text{Number of Shares} - \text{Transaction Costs}$$

Market surveillance and risk management have also benefited from technological advancements. Regulatory bodies now employ sophisticated surveillance systems to detect and prevent market manipulation and fraudulent activities. These systems analyze trading patterns to identify suspicious behavior, such as insider trading or front running. Additionally, advanced risk management software enables firms to monitor their exposure to different types of risk in real-time, ensuring compliance with regulatory requirements and safeguarding against market shocks.

The impact of technology extends beyond the front office to the operational infrastructures of financial institutions. The adoption of blockchain technology, for instance, promises to enhance the efficiency and security of post-trade processes. By providing a transparent and immutable ledger, blockchain can streamline settlement procedures, reduce counterparty risk, and lower transaction costs. Smart contracts, which are self-executing contracts with the terms directly written into code, can further automate and secure the execution of complex financial agreements.

However, the rapid pace of technological change also presents challenges and risks. The increasing reliance on automated systems raises concerns about systemic risk, as technical glitches or algorithmic errors can trigger market disruptions. The Flash Crash of 2010, where the Dow Jones Industrial Average plunged nearly 1,000 points in minutes, highlights the potential for technology-induced volatility. Cybersecurity threats pose another significant risk, necessitating robust protections to safeguard sensitive financial data and ensure the integrity of trading systems.

Looking ahead, emerging technologies such as artificial intelligence (AI) and quantum computing hold the potential to further transform market microstructure. AI algorithms can enhance predictive analytics by processing unstructured data sources, such as news articles and social media sentiment, to generate trading signals. Quantum computing promises exponential improvements in computational speed, enabling the solving of complex optimization problems that are currently infeasible.

In light of these advancements, the role of technology in modern markets is both profound and multifaceted. It not only alters the mechanics of trading but also reshapes the competitive landscape, regulatory environment, and the nature of market participation. As technology continues to evolve, staying abreast of these developments is imperative for both market practitioners and policymakers to navigate the increasingly complex and dynamic financial ecosystem.

Chapter 2

Order Types and Order Books

This chapter explores the variety of order types available in financial markets, such as market orders, limit orders, and stop orders, and explains their distinct functionalities and use cases. It delves into the dynamics of order books, detailing how buy and sell orders are matched and executed. The chapter further examines the impact of different order types on market behavior and liquidity, providing insights into the strategic considerations traders must account for when placing orders. Understanding these elements is crucial for navigating the intricacies of market interactions and optimizing trading performance.

2.1 Types of Orders

In the financial markets, understanding the variety of order types is fundamental to executing effective trading strategies. Each order type has distinct characteristics, advantages, and suitable scenarios, influencing both the trader's approach and the market's behavior. We'll cover the primary order types: market orders, limit orders, and stop orders, as well as introduce various conditional and specialized orders that enhance trading flexibility.

Market orders are the simplest form of trade execution. A market order instructs the broker to buy or sell an asset immediately at the best available current price. This type of order prioritizes speed over price control, making it beneficial in situations where prompt execution is critical. However, market orders are subject to slippage, meaning the execution price could differ from the expected price, especially in volatile markets.

Limit orders, on the other hand, provide more control over the execution price. A limit order specifies the maximum price at which a trader is willing to buy or the minimum price for selling. These orders are placed in the order book and only executed if the market reaches the specified price. While limit orders may not be filled immediately—or at all—they protect traders from adverse price movements and can be intended for strategic entry or exit points.

Stop orders act as risk management tools. A stop order becomes a market order once a predetermined price, known as the stop price, is reached. Stop orders come in two main forms: stop-loss and stop-limit. A stop-loss order aims to limit a trader's loss by triggering a market order to sell an asset when its price falls to a specific level. Conversely, a stop-limit order becomes a limit order at the stop price, combining the price control of limit orders with the exit strategy of stop orders.

Beyond these basic types, several conditional orders offer additional sophistication. For instance, a bracket order, often used in conjunction with limit orders, encompasses a primary order and two opposite-side exit orders, typically a profit-taking limit order and a stop-loss order. This ensures that once the primary order is executed, the exits manage the trade automatically within predefined price brackets.

Moreover, advanced traders might use an iceberg order to minimize market impact by only showing a small portion of the total order size in the order book, hiding the rest until the visible part is executed. This technique is useful in maintaining discretion, particularly for large volume trades.

Another notable order type is the good-till-canceled (GTC) order, which remains active until the trader decides to cancel it or the order is executed, avoiding the need for daily renewal. Variants such as day orders, which expire at the end of the trading day if not executed, and fill-or-kill (FOK) orders, which must be executed in their entirety immediately or not at all, offer additional control over the lifespan and execution conditions of trades.

For algorithmic traders, the all-or-none (AON) order ensures that the entire order is executed in a single transaction, preventing partial fills which might disrupt complex trading strategies. Similarly, the immediate-or-cancel (IOC) order specifies that any unfilled portion of the order should be canceled if it cannot be executed immediately.

Understanding the nuances of these order types and how they can be effectively employed is essential for tailoring trading strategies to specific market conditions. Whether seeking immediate execution or precise control over price, utilizing the appropriate order type can significantly influence trading outcomes. As we move deeper into the mechanics and strategic implications of these orders, the critical role they play within the market microstructure will become increasingly apparent.

2.2 Market Orders vs. Limit Orders

Market orders and limit orders are two fundamental types of orders that traders use extensively in financial markets. Understanding the distinct characteristics, advantages, and potential pitfalls of these order types is crucial for effective trading. This section provides a comprehensive exploration of market orders and limit orders, detailing their functionalities, appropriate use cases, and strategic considerations.

Market orders are designed to execute immediately at the best available price. When a trader submits a market order, it signals a willingness to buy or sell a security at current market prices, regardless of any small price changes that may occur during execution. The primary advantage of market orders is their speed. They are typically prioritized for execution over other order types, ensuring that the trader can enter or exit a position promptly. This speed is beneficial in scenarios where immediate execution is more critical than the exact price obtained, such as during highly volatile market conditions or when rapidly responding to breaking news.

However, the certainty of execution that market orders provide comes at the cost of price uncertainty, especially in less liquid markets. Market orders can be executed at multiple price levels, particularly if the size of the order exceeds the quantity available at the best current bid or ask price. This can lead to a phenomenon known as "slippage", where the final execution price differs from the expected market price at the time the order was placed. For instance, in a rapidly moving market or one with low liquidity, the trader may receive a significantly worse price than anticipated.

To illustrate the mechanics of market orders, consider the following example:

Suppose a trader wants to buy 100 shares of XYZ Corporation. The current best ask price is $50.00, but only 50 shares are available at that price. The remaining 50 shares may be filled at higher ask prices, say, $50.05 or $50.10, depending on the volume and order flow in the order book. The trader will not know the exact average price paid until the order is fully executed. This example underscores the importance of understanding market depth and potential slippage when placing large market orders.

On the other hand, limit orders allow traders to define the maximum price they are willing to pay when buying or the minimum price they are willing to accept when selling. These orders are designed to provide price certainty by executing only at the specified limit price or better. Unlike market orders, limit orders do not guarantee immediate execution. Instead, they enter the order book and will only execute if the market price meets the specified limit price.

The advantage of limit orders lies in their ability to control execution prices, which makes them particularly useful in less liquid markets or when trading larger positions. By specifying a limit price, traders can avoid slippage and ensure that they do not pay more, or receive less, than they intended. This price control is invaluable during periods of market volatility or thin trading volumes, where rapid price movements can otherwise lead to unfavorable trade executions.

For example, if a trader wants to buy 100 shares of XYZ Corporation but only wants to pay up to $50.00 per share, they can place a limit order with a buy limit price of $50.00. The order will only execute if the ask price drops to $50.00 or lower. If the market price never reaches $50.00, the order will remain unfilled. This mechanism allows the trader to have maximum control over the transaction price but introduces the risk of the order not being executed if the market does not move favorably.

When comparing market orders to limit orders, several strategic considerations emerge. Traders must weigh the trade-offs between execution speed and price control. Market orders are preferable when the urgency of trade execution outweighs concerns about the exact transaction price. For instance, during significant market events or when capitalizing on a fleeting opportunity, the certainty of immediate trade execution can be more critical than securing the best possible price.

Alternatively, limit orders are appropriate when price precision is paramount. Traders can use limit orders to set specific entry or exit points, particularly in less liquid markets or when dealing with large order sizes. This strategy helps to mitigate the impact of slippage and unfavorable price movements, providing more predictable trading outcomes.

Algorithmic traders often incorporate both market and limit orders into their trading systems, depending on the strategy and market conditions. For instance, high-frequency trading algorithms may favor market orders during periods of high liquidity to ensure rapid execution, whereas execution algorithms designed to obtain the best possible average price over a period may primarily use limit orders.

In conclusion, both market orders and limit orders serve critical roles in the trading ecosystem. Market orders provide the benefit of rapid execution but at the risk of uncertain pricing, making them ideal for time-sensitive trades. Limit orders offer price control, at the potential expense of execution certainty, making them suitable for traders prioritizing price precision. Understanding these order types and adeptly applying them in varying market conditions is fundamental to optimizing trading performance and achieving strategic trading goals.

2.3 Stop Orders and Conditional Orders

Stop orders and conditional orders play a critical role in the strategic toolkit of traders. These order types can help manage risk, automate trading strategies, and react swiftly to market movements when specific conditions are met. Understanding the intricacies of stop orders and conditional orders is essential for optimizing trades and managing a portfolio effectively.

A stop order is an instruction to buy or sell a security once its price moves past a specific point, ensuring a higher probability of achieving a predetermined entry or exit price. There are two primary types of stop orders: stop-loss orders and stop-limit orders.

A stop-loss order triggers a market order once the stop price is reached. For example, if you own a stock currently trading at $50 and place a stop-loss order at $45, the stock will automatically be sold at the best available price once it drops to $45, limiting potential losses. This type of order is an essential tool for risk management, allowing traders to set a predefined level at which they are no longer willing to sustain further losses.

$$\text{Stop-Loss Order: Sell if Price} \leq \text{Stop Price}$$

Alternatively, a stop-limit order combines features of both stop and limit orders. This type of order requires two price points: the stop price (which triggers the order) and the limit price (which specifies the lowest acceptable price for the trade). For example, if you place a stop-limit order with a stop price of $45 and a limit of $44, the order will only be executed if the price falls to $45 but will not be sold for less than $44. This precision can provide more control over trade execution but carries the risk that the order may not be filled if the market price falls rapidly past the limit price.

$$\text{Stop-Limit Order: Sell if Price} \leq \text{Stop Price and} \geq \text{Limit Price}$$

Conditional orders extend beyond the basic stop orders by adding more sophisticated criteria for trade execution. These orders include one-cancels-the-other (OCO) orders and bracket orders.

An OCO order involves two orders simultaneously, where the execution of one automatically cancels the other. This strategy is beneficial when a trader aims to enter the market when certain conditions are met or exit to capture gains or limit losses. For instance, an OCO order might combine a buy stop order and a sell stop order; if one part of the order is triggered, the other is canceled, thus automating the trading decision.

$$\text{OCO Order:} \begin{cases} \text{Execute Order A} \\ \text{Cancel Order B} \end{cases} \text{or} \begin{cases} \text{Execute Order B} \\ \text{Cancel Order A} \end{cases}$$

Bracket orders include three components: an entry order, a profit-taking limit order, and a stop-loss order. When the entry order is filled, the profit-taking and stop-loss orders are automatically placed, creating a "bracket" around the current market price. This approach ensures that profits are taken at a desired level while also protecting from significant losses.

$$\text{Bracket Order:} \begin{cases} \text{Entry Order} \\ \text{Profit-Taking Limit Order} & \text{(Above Entry Price)} \\ \text{Stop-Loss Order} & \text{(Below Entry Price)} \end{cases}$$

These orders help in managing trades with greater precision and control. Given the volatility and fast-moving nature of financial markets, being able to set predefined conditions ensures that trades execute in accordance with a trader's strategic objectives. This automation reduces the need for constant monitoring and helps in maintaining emotional discipline, preventing rash decisions driven by panic or greed.

By incorporating stop and conditional orders, traders can create a structured framework within which they operate, guided by predetermined rules and risk parameters. This not only optimizes their potential for returns but also ensures consistency in their trading approach, aligning with broader financial goals and risk tolerance levels.

2.4   Understanding Order Books

An order book is a continuously updated record of buy and sell orders in a financial market, organized by price levels. It reflects the current demand and supply for a particular asset, enabling traders to make informed decisions based on market depth and liquidity. By understanding how order books operate, traders gain insights into market sentiment and can better time their trades.

At its core, the order book lists two main types of orders: buy orders (bids) and sell orders (asks). Each order is tagged with a price and quantity, showing the highest price buyers are willing to pay and the lowest price sellers are willing to accept. The comparison between these two figures is crucial in establishing the bid-ask spread, which is the difference between the highest bid and the lowest ask price.

When considering how order books function, it's important to grasp several foundational elements:

Bid and Ask Prices:

$$\text{Bid Price} = \max\{\text{price of all buy orders}\}$$

$$\text{Ask Price} = \min\{\text{price of all sell orders}\}$$

The bid-ask spread can be defined as:

$$\text{Bid-Ask Spread} = \text{Ask Price} - \text{Bid Price}$$

A narrower spread often indicates a more liquid market, as it implies a tighter consensus on asset valuation between buyers and sellers.

Market Depth: Market depth illustrates the quantity of buy and sell orders at different price levels. A deeper market generally signifies higher liquidity, reducing the likelihood of significant price fluctuations from large trades. Market depth can be visually represented through a depth chart, which plots cumulative bid and ask sizes against prices.

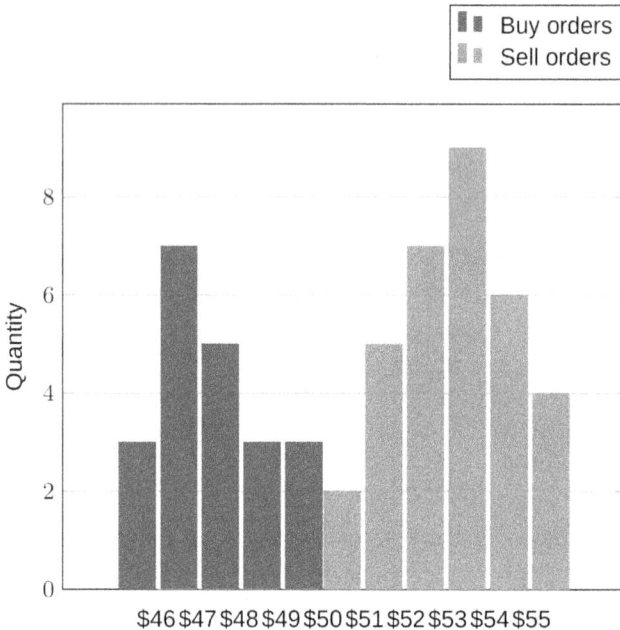

In the depth chart example above, the cumulative buy orders (bids) are plotted on the left, showing the total volume at each price level below the current bid price. Similarly, cumulative sell orders (asks) are plotted on the right for prices above the current ask price.

Order Matching: Order matching in the order book is handled through specific rules established by the exchange, primarily aiming to ensure fair trading. When a new order is placed, it is immediately compared against existing orders in the book. If a match is found based on price and quantity, a trade occurs, and the respective orders are removed from the book.

For instance, if the highest existing bid is $50 for 100 shares and a new sell order is placed at $50 for at least 100 shares, the trade will be executed at that price. This process involves the principles of price-time priority, where orders at a better price (higher bids or lower asks) take precedence, and among orders at the same price, those placed earlier get matched first.

A simple algorithmic flow for order matching can be described as follows:

```
for each newly placed order:
    if 'buy' order:
        find the lowest ask price in the order book
        if new order price >= lowest ask price:
            execute trade at lowest ask price
            adjust order quantities in the book
        else:
            add new order to the bid side of the order book
    if 'sell' order:
        find the highest bid price in the order book
        if new order price <= highest bid price:
            execute trade at highest bid price
            adjust order quantities in the book
        else:
            add new order to the ask side of the order book
```

Understanding market depth and order matching is essential for deciphering the mechanics behind order books. Familiarity with these concepts enables traders to anticipate market movements, manage transactions efficiently, and employ sophisticated strategies, such as placing iceberg orders (orders with partially hidden size) to minimize market impact.

Order Book Transparency: The extent of visibility into the order book varies with each trading venue. Full transparency, as seen in some exchanges, allows traders to view the entire set of bid and ask orders. However, in many markets, especially those with high-frequency trading or dark pools, only the best bid and ask prices are visible, obscuring the full depth of the order book. This partial visibility can challenge retail traders, as institutional participants might possess more comprehensive data through direct market access.

In summary, order books encapsulate the collective market interest and provide invaluable data for making informed trading decisions. By continuously monitoring the evolving landscape of buy and sell orders, traders enhance their ability to interpret and navigate the intricacies of the financial markets, thereby optimizing their trading performance.

2.5   The Mechanics of Order Matching

In the labyrinthine world of financial markets, the process of order matching serves as the invisible hand that orchestrates the harmonious exchange of securities between buyers and sellers. Understanding the mechanics of order matching is pivotal for any trader aiming to navigate the complexities of market operations effectively.

When an order is placed, it doesn't magically result in the immediate transaction of securities. Instead, it enters an ecosystem where it will be matched against other orders based on predetermined rules and priorities. A key player in this ecosystem is the *order book*, an electronic ledger that records and organizes orders. The order book is typically divided into two sides: bids (buy orders) and asks (sell orders).

The first principle to grasp is the priority hierarchy that determines the order in which trades are executed. In most contemporary trading venues, orders are matched based on a combination of *price priority* and *time priority*. Price priority dictates that the highest bid and the lowest ask receive the first opportunity for execution. Within the same price category, time priority gives precedence to the orders that arrived first.

Let's delve further with an illustrative example. Suppose the current best bid for a stock is $100 and the best ask is $101. If a new buy order comes in at $101, it will immediately execute against the best ask, resulting in a trade. On the other hand, if a buy order is placed at $100 or lower, it will join the queue of existing bids, waiting for a matching sell order at that price level or better.

The order book's role is not static. It continually evolves as new orders are added, matched, or canceled. This dynamic environment can be represented by the following example of an order book snapshot:

Price	Bid Size	Ask Size
102	0	200
101	0	300
100	500	0
99	400	0
98	600	0

Table 2.1: Order Book Snapshot

In the table above, the highest bid is at $100 with a size of 500 shares, and the lowest ask is at $101 with a size of 300 shares. If a market order to buy 200 shares is submitted, it will execute against the 300 shares available at the best ask price of $101, thus reducing the ask size at $101 to 100 shares.

Algorithmic trading systems, also known as engines, play a significant role in the mechanics of order matching. These systems are designed to process orders with minimal latency, ensuring that time priority is respected to the microsecond level. Such precision is vital in high-frequency trading (HFT) where even a millisecond lead can offer substantial advantages.

Moreover, different markets may employ distinct matching algorithms. For instance, the *pro-rata* matching algorithm differs from the simple price-time priority by distributing the matching of orders proportionally based on the order size. This method is often seen in derivatives markets where it facilitates larger transactions by splitting them proportionally amongst the existing orders at a given price level.

Another mechanism often seen in practice is the *auction process*. Periodic auctions, such as the opening and closing auctions, can help establish a fair market price by consolidating liquidity at specific times. During these auctions, orders accumulate over a short period instead of being immediately matched, resulting in a single bulk match at the auction price.

The stability and fairness of order matching mechanisms are pivotal for maintaining market confidence. Anomalies such as *flash crashes* often highlight the fragility of these systems under extreme conditions and underscore the importance of robust algorithm design and regulatory oversight. Ensuring that the order matching process is transparent and efficient is a continual challenge for market operators and regulators alike.

Seasoned traders often exploit their knowledge of order matching mechanics to optimize their strategies. For instance, by analyzing the depth and structure of the order book, traders can anticipate *slippage*—the difference between the expected price of a trade and the actual price obtained due to market movement. Managing slippage is crucial for executing large orders without significantly impacting market prices.

The mechanics of order matching are a testament to the intricate design and technology underpinning modern financial markets. Mastering the subtleties of how orders are matched not only enhances one's strategic trading skills but also provides a deeper appreciation of the market's operational integrity.

2.6   Order Book Dynamics

Understanding the dynamics of order books is essential for traders who aim to navigate the market with precision and efficiency. An order book is a real-time, constantly changing list of buy and sell orders in a given market. It provides an up-to-date snapshot of market sentiment and liquidity, reflecting the collective actions and intentions of all market participants. This section will explain the essential aspects of order book dynamics, including how the order book is structured, the importance of depth and liquidity, and how traders can interpret and leverage this information to optimize their trading strategies.

In a typical order book for a single security, orders are displayed in a structured format with bid (buy) orders on one side and ask (sell) orders on the other. The bids are arranged from the highest price downwards, and the asks are arranged from the lowest price upwards. This structure allows traders to quickly gauge the highest price someone is willing to pay for the security and the lowest price at which someone is willing to sell it. The price at which the highest bid and the lowest ask meet is called the *best bid* and *best ask*, respectively. The difference between these two prices is known as the *bid-ask spread*.

- **Depth and Liquidity:** Depth refers to the volume of orders available at each price level within the order book. A market is often considered deep if there are substantial volumes of orders close to the current best bid and ask prices. Liquidity, on the other hand, refers to how quickly and easily a security can be bought or sold without causing a significant impact on its price. Highly liquid markets typically exhibit narrow bid-ask spreads and substantial order book depth.

$$\text{Market Depth} = \sum_{i=1}^{n} V_i$$

where V_i represents the volume of orders at each price level i, and n is the total number of price levels considered. For a market to be highly liquid, this summation should yield a large volume, indicating that there is plenty of interest in trading the security across different prices.

The depth of an order book can have substantial implications for trading strategies. For instance, in a market with shallow depth, a

36

large market order could significantly impact the security's price, leading to slippage. Conversely, in a deep market, the same order would likely be filled more quickly and with a lesser impact on price, offering better execution quality.

- **Visualizing Order Books:** Order books are often visualized using depth charts or order book heat maps. A depth chart plots the cumulative volume of buy and sell orders against their respective prices. The chart usually features two lines: the bid line, representing cumulative buy orders, and the ask line, representing cumulative sell orders.

  This graphical representation helps traders identify critical price levels where significant volumes of orders are clustered, allowing them to gauge potential support and resistance levels in the market.

  Order book heat maps, on the other hand, display the volume of orders at different prices using color patterns, where more vibrant areas represent higher volumes. This visualization can help traders quickly see where liquidity is concentrated and identify potential areas of interest for placing trades.

- **Order Book Imbalance and Market Impact:** Order book imbalance refers to the difference in volume between buy and sell orders at various price levels. This imbalance can signal potential market direction. A significant imbalance with a greater volume of buy orders relative to sell orders might indicate bullish sentiments, while an imbalance in the opposite direction suggests bearish sentiments.

$$\text{Order Book Imbalance} = \frac{\text{Volume of Buy Orders} - \text{Volume of Sell Orders}}{\text{Total Volume}}$$

Analyzing order book imbalance allows traders to anticipate short-term price movements and adjust their strategies accordingly. For example, a persistent imbalance favoring buy orders might encourage traders to adopt a long position, expecting upward price movement.

The market impact of orders is another crucial aspect of order book dynamics. Large orders can move the price significantly, especially in less liquid markets. Traders often use the *Implementation Shortfall* method to measure market impact.

Implementation Shortfall = Execution Price − Initial Price

By understanding potential market impact, traders can implement strategies like slicing their orders into smaller pieces, known as *iceberg orders*, or using algorithmic trading techniques to mitigate adverse price movements.

As we delve deeper into order book dynamics, it becomes evident how these elements interplay to influence market behavior. Grasping these dynamics equips traders with the necessary tools to navigate the market efficiently, making informed decisions that account for depth, liquidity, and potential market impact. Recognizing patterns within the order book, understanding the significance of visual tools, and anticipating price movements through imbalance analysis are essential skills that, when mastered, enhance a trader's ability to execute superior trading strategies.

2.7   Impact of Different Order Types on Market Behavior

Understanding the impact of different order types on market behavior is instrumental in crafting effective trading strategies. Market orders, limit orders, and stop orders each have unique characteristics that influence their interaction with market liquidity and price formation. This section delves into these impacts, offering a nuanced view of how various orders shape the trading environment.

When a trader places a **market order**, they are instructing the market to buy or sell immediately at the best available price. The urgency of execution prioritizes speed over price, which can lead to price slippage, particularly in less liquid markets. Market orders move the market by consuming liquidity. For instance, a large market buy order can significantly increase the price by filling multiple levels of the order book, creating upward momentum. Conversely, a market sell order can drive prices down by sweeping through the available bid orders.

In mathematical terms, if we denote the market price at time t as P_t, then the price impact ΔP due to a market order of size Q can be approximated as:

$$\Delta P \approx \lambda Q$$

where λ is a liquidity parameter that captures the market's depth and resiliency. High λ values indicate a shallower market where large orders create more significant price disruptions.

On the other hand, **limit orders** define the price at which a trader is willing to buy or sell, effectively adding liquidity to the market. These orders are queued in the order book until they are matched with a corresponding opposite side order. Limit orders contribute to the market's depth by providing executable prices. However, their impact on market behavior is more passive than market orders since they do not initiate trades immediately.

One critical aspect to consider is the *spread*, which is the difference between the highest bid and the lowest ask price. Limit orders help to narrow the spread over time as more competitive pricing comes into play. For example, if the spread is initially wide, new limit orders posted closer to the current price levels encourage tighter spreads, enhancing market efficiency.

$$\text{Spread} = P_{\text{Ask}} - P_{\text{Bid}}$$

An influx of limit buy orders can push bids closer to the ask price, reducing the spread, and vice versa for limit sell orders.

Stop orders and conditional orders add another layer of complexity. These orders activate once specific conditions are met, making them a strategic tool for managing risks and entry points. For example, a stop-loss order is placed to sell a security once its price drops to a specific level, protecting against further downside:

$$P_{\text{Stop-Loss}} = P_{\text{Threshold}}$$

When the market price reaches the stop-loss threshold, the order converts to a market order, which can exacerbate price moves, particularly in volatile conditions. Conversely, stop-buy orders can serve as breakout triggers, buying at a higher price if upward momentum is confirmed.

The introduction of stop orders can lead to phenomena like *stop hunting*, where more prominent players push prices to trigger cascading stop orders, thereby creating abrupt price movements followed by quick reversals. Such activity highlights the importance of situational awareness and the strategic placement of stop orders to mitigate adverse effects.

In sum, different order types create distinct patterns in market behavior. Market orders directly influence price levels and momentum by consuming liquidity and causing immediate price adjustments. Limit orders enhance market depth and reduce spreads, contributing to a more stable and efficient trading environment. Stop orders introduce conditional dynamics, often amplifying volatility around key price levels.

Through understanding these mechanics, traders can better anticipate market movements and optimize their order placement to align with their strategic objectives. By analyzing how different order types interact with the order book, market participants can gain insights into market sentiment, liquidity provisions, and potential price trajectories, thus enhancing their capacity to navigate the intricate landscape of financial markets.

Chapter 3

Price Discovery and Formation

This chapter delves into the mechanisms of price discovery, highlighting how market prices are determined through the interplay of supply and demand. It examines the roles of fundamental analysis, technical analysis, and external events in shaping price formation. The impact of market sentiment and behavioral finance on price movements is explored, alongside a discussion of the Efficient Market Hypothesis and its implications for price accuracy and predictability. Understanding these processes is essential for making informed trading decisions and accurately interpreting market signals.

3.1 Concept of Price Discovery

Price discovery is a fundamental concept that lies at the heart of financial markets, embodying the process through which the equilibrium price of an asset is determined. This mechanism involves the continuous interaction between buyers and sellers, each bringing their own information, expectations, and constraints to the marketplace. In its essence, price discovery reflects the collective knowledge and sentiment of market participants, amalgamating diverse pieces of information to form a coherent and actionable price.

To understand price discovery, it is important to consider the dynamics between supply and demand as well as the information embedded in their movements. When supply equals demand, the market is said to be in equilibrium. However, reaching this state is not a static process but a dynamic one, influenced by a multitude of factors, including macroeconomic indicators, corporate earnings, geopolitical events, and investor psychology.

One core aspect of price discovery is the concept of market efficiency. A market is considered efficient if prices fully reflect all available information. In such a scenario, it becomes challenging to consistently achieve returns above the market average, as prices already incorporate the knowledge and expectations of all participants. This idea, encapsulated in the Efficient Market Hypothesis (EMH), is foundational for understanding how quickly and accurately prices can adjust to new information.

Price discovery occurs on multiple timeframes and through various market structures. For instance, high-frequency traders may impact price discovery in the very short term through their rapid trades, while long-term investors may influence prices through fundamental valuations. The diversity of time horizons among market participants contributes to a more robust and layered price discovery process, where short-term noise and long-term trends are woven together.

Another critical element in price discovery is the role of market makers and liquidity providers. These entities facilitate trading by providing quotes for buying and selling securities, thus ensuring that there is always a counterparty available for transactions. Their activities help narrow the bid-ask spread, increasing market liquidity and enabling smoother price transitions.

The order book, which records all buy and sell orders, is a vital tool in understanding price discovery. It provides transparency regarding the depth and breadth of the market, showing the quantities available at various price levels. Market participants can adjust their strategies based on this information, thereby influencing the price discovery process.

Moreover, price discovery is not solely a function of rational calculation but also of behavioral factors. Market sentiment, driven by emotions such as fear and greed, can lead to price movements that temporarily deviate from fundamental values. Understanding the psychological underpinnings of market behavior allows traders and investors to anticipate potential overreactions or underreactions to news and events.

In algorithmic trading, price discovery is enhanced through the use of sophisticated models that analyze vast amounts of data in real time. These algorithms can detect patterns and make trading decisions more quickly than human traders, thus contributing to the continuous adjustment of prices. The integration of artificial intelligence and machine learning further refines this process, allowing for more nuanced and adaptive strategies.

To illustrate the concept of price discovery, consider the initial public offering (IPO) of a company. During an IPO, the company and its underwriters set an initial price range based on various factors, including market conditions, financial performance, and investor demand. As the stock begins trading, the actual price discovery occurs as market participants start buying and selling shares. The initial price may adjust rapidly as the market assimilates new information and reaches a consensus on the stock's value.

Understanding the concept of price discovery enables traders and investors to make informed decisions by recognizing the underlying forces that drive market prices. By appreciating the interactions between supply, demand, information flow, and market behavior, one can better navigate the complexities of financial markets and enhance their trading and investing strategies.

3.2   Role of Supply and Demand

The dynamics of supply and demand are fundamental to the concept of price discovery. Understanding these dynamics allows traders and investors to interpret and anticipate price movements more effectively. At its core, price determination in financial markets operates on the basic economic principle where the price of an asset is established at the point where supply meets demand. This section delves into the intricate mechanisms of how supply and demand interact and influence market prices.

Demand Side Mechanics:

The demand for an asset is driven by the aggregate of all market participants who are willing and able to purchase the asset at various price levels. When examining demand, it's crucial to consider factors such as:

- *Investor Sentiment*: Positive sentiment can increase demand as investors anticipate rising prices and potential profits.

- *Economic Indicators*: Strong economic indicators such as GDP growth, low unemployment rates, and rising consumer confidence can boost demand as they signal a robust economy.

- *Interest Rates*: Lower interest rates reduce the cost of borrowing, encouraging investment in higher-yielding assets, thereby increasing demand.

- *Market News and Events*: Favorable news, such as positive earnings reports or regulatory approvals, can heighten demand for specific assets.

Mathematically, we can represent the demand function Q_D as:

$$Q_D = f(P, Y, r, E)$$

where P represents the price of the asset, Y encompasses various economic indicators, r stands for the interest rates, and E denotes investor expectations. This equation encapsulates how changes in these variables can shift the demand curve.

Supply Side Mechanics:

Conversely, supply reflects the total quantity of an asset that market participants are willing and able to sell at varying price levels. Factors influencing supply include:

- *Production Costs*: For commodities and goods, higher production costs can restrain supply as firms need higher prices to cover expenses.

- *Market Conditions*: In equity markets, a company's decision to issue new shares can increase supply.

- *Technological Advances*: Improvements in production technology can increase supply by reducing costs and improving efficiency.

- *Government Policies*: Regulations such as tariffs, taxes, and quotas can significantly impact supply levels.

The supply function Q_S can be formulated as:

$$Q_S = g(P, C, T, G)$$

where P is the price, C includes production costs, T accounts for technological factors, and G represents government policies. These components interact to determine the quantity supplied at different price points.

Market Equilibrium:

The intersection of the supply and demand curves denotes the market equilibrium, where the quantity supplied equals the quantity demanded. This equilibrium price is the market's consensus value for the asset at a given point in time. Determination of this equilibrium requires balancing the factors affecting both sides of the equation.

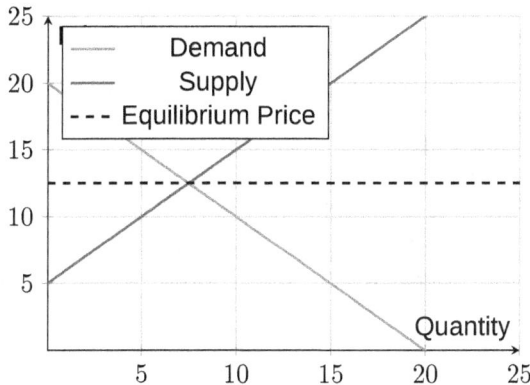

In this illustrative chart, the demand curve slopes downward, indicating that as the price decreases, the quantity demanded increases. Conversely, the supply curve slopes upward, suggesting that higher prices incentivize producers to supply more of the asset. The equilibrium point balances these forces.

Shifts in Supply and Demand:

While the equilibrium price provides a snapshot of the current market state, the market is dynamic, and any changes in the underlying determinants of supply or demand can lead to shifts in these curves. For example:

- An innovation that lowers production costs can shift the supply curve to the right, resulting in a lower equilibrium price.

45

- An economic boom can shift the demand curve to the right as higher incomes increase the purchasing power of consumers, leading to a higher equilibrium price.

- Policy changes such as subsidies can reduce costs for producers, thereby increasing supply and shifting the supply curve rightwards.

- A negative economic forecast may shift the demand curve leftwards as consumers become more conservative with their spending, reducing the equilibrium price.

These shifts can be visualized graphically, where the new intersection of the supply and demand curves represents the adjusted market equilibrium. It is crucial for traders to monitor these shifts closely, as they signify changes in market conditions that can present profitable trading opportunities.

The interaction between supply and demand is essential for understanding price movements in financial markets. By examining the intricate factors that influence supply and demand and their subsequent impact on market equilibrium, traders can enhance their market analysis and improve their ability to make informed trading decisions. This comprehension forms a cornerstone in the broader context of price discovery, enabling a clearer and more strategic approach to navigating the complexities of market pricing.

3.3   Fundamental Analysis in Price Formation

Fundamental analysis plays a central role in the price formation process, underpinning the valuation of financial assets through a comprehensive examination of economic, financial, and other qualitative and quantitative factors. This approach seeks to determine the intrinsic value of a security, providing investors insight into whether a stock is undervalued or overvalued compared to its current market price.

At its core, fundamental analysis involves delving into key aspects such as a company's financial statements, industry conditions, economic indicators, and broader market environments. The goal is to formulate a clearer picture of the asset's true worth and to identify potential investment opportunities.

Financial Statements Analysis

A thorough examination of a company's financial statements is a foundational aspect of fundamental analysis. Understanding the income statement, balance sheet, and cash flow statement is pivotal. These documents reveal critical information about a company's profitability, financial health, and cash-generating capabilities.

The income statement provides insights into revenue, expenses, and net income over a specific period. Analysts look for trends in earnings, profit margins, and revenue growth to assess a company's operational efficiency and potential for future profits.

The balance sheet offers a snapshot of a company's assets, liabilities, and shareholders' equity at a given point in time. Key metrics derived from the balance sheet, such as the current ratio and debt-to-equity ratio, help in evaluating a company's financial stability and leverage.

The cash flow statement highlights cash inflows and outflows from operating, investing, and financing activities. Positive cash flows from operations are a strong indicator of a company's ability to generate sufficient cash to sustain and grow its operations without relying on external financing.

Ratios and Valuation Metrics

Ratios are indispensable tools in fundamental analysis, allowing for comparative assessments across different companies and industry benchmarks. Commonly used ratios include the Price-to-Earnings (P/E) ratio, Price-to-Book (P/B) ratio, and Dividend Yield.

The P/E ratio measures a company's current share price relative to its per-share earnings. A high P/E ratio might indicate that a stock is overvalued, or that investors expect high growth rates in the future. Conversely, a low P/E ratio could suggest that the stock is undervalued or that the company is experiencing difficulties.

The P/B ratio compares a company's market value to its book value, offering insights into how investors value the company's net assets. This ratio can reveal whether a stock is trading above or below its actual value on the company's books.

The Dividend Yield, expressed as a percentage, indicates how much a company pays out in dividends each year relative to its stock price. This metric is particularly important for income-focused investors looking for steady income streams from their investments.

Macroeconomic Indicators

Understanding the broader economic environment is crucial to fundamental analysis. Macroeconomic indicators such as GDP growth rates, inflation rates, employment statistics, and interest rates can significantly impact a company's performance and, consequently, its stock price.

For instance, higher interest rates can increase borrowing costs for companies, potentially squeezing profit margins and reducing investment in growth initiatives. Conversely, lower interest rates might encourage expansion and capital investment, driving future earnings growth.

Industry Conditions

Assessing the competitive landscape within an industry helps in understanding how external forces might influence a company's future prospects. Industry analysis examines factors like market size, growth potential, competitive intensity, and regulatory environment.

Porter's Five Forces framework is a valuable tool for industry analysis. It evaluates competitive rivalry, the threat of new entrants, the power of suppliers, the power of customers, and the threat of substitute products or services. An industry characterized by high competitive rivalry may lead to lower profit margins, while an industry with significant entry barriers might allow for sustained profitability for incumbent firms.

Qualitative Analysis

Qualitative aspects such as management quality, brand strength, and corporate governance also significantly influence a company's valuation. Experienced and competent management teams are better positioned to navigate economic challenges and capitalize on growth opportunities.

Corporate governance practices, including board structure, shareholder rights, and transparency, play a crucial role in ensuring that management's interests are aligned with those of shareholders, thereby enhancing long-term shareholder value.

Significance in Price Formation

Fundamental analysis seeks to understand the actual value drivers of a company, advocating that market prices will, in the long term, converge with intrinsic value. Market prices fluctuate due to short-term noise and investor sentiment, but fundamentally sound companies tend to achieve price corrections that reflect their true worth over time.

This method can also be instrumental in identifying mispriced securities.

By identifying discrepancies between market valuations and intrinsic values, fundamental analysis provides avenues for profitable trades. For instance, if a stock's market price is significantly below its intrinsic value, it may represent a buying opportunity, anticipating that the market will eventually recognize and correct the undervaluation.

Incorporating fundamental analysis into trading strategies enhances the ability to make informed decisions, particularly in differentiating between short-lived market trends and enduring value. The depth and thoroughness of fundamental analysis provide a robust foundation for long-term investment success, contributing significantly to the overall process of price discovery and formation in the financial markets.

Understanding these nuanced elements and their interconnectedness enriches an investor's competency in navigating the complex landscapes of trading and investing. This depth of knowledge not only informs better decision-making but also builds confidence in interpreting market signals and capitalizing on opportunities within the ever-evolving markets.

3.4   Technical Analysis in Price Formation

Technical analysis is a crucial methodology in the process of price formation, focusing on statistical trends derived from trading activities, including price movement and volume. Unlike fundamental analysis, which examines a company's financial health and economic variables, technical analysis relies on interpreting historical price patterns to predict future price movements. This approach is premised on the belief that market prices reflect all information, even when that information includes investor emotions and market psychology.

At the core of technical analysis is the assumption that historical price trends tend to repeat due to the collective behavior of market participants. This behavior, whether rational or irrational, leads to identifiable patterns and trends over time, enabling technical analysts to make probabilistic forecasts about future price direction.

Price Charts and Patterns

Price charts are fundamental tools in technical analysis, providing visual representations of asset price movements over specific periods. Common chart types include line charts, bar charts, and candlestick charts.

Candlestick charts, in particular, are highly valued for their ability to display open, high, low, and close prices within a single candle, providing a comprehensive view of the trading period. Each candle indicates how the market has performed, capturing the sentiment and tendencies of market participants.

Patterns within these charts, such as head and shoulders, double tops and bottoms, and flags, are associated with shifts in market sentiment and potential reversals or continuations in price trends. For instance, a head and shoulders pattern often signals a reversal in an uptrend, indicating a potential shift to a downtrend.

Technical Indicators

Technical indicators are mathematical calculations based on historical price, volume, or open interest data. They are designed to identify significant areas of price movement and aid in forecasting future price action. Some of the commonly used indicators include:

- *Moving Averages*: Used to smooth out price data and identify the direction of the trend. The Simple Moving Average (SMA) and the Exponential Moving Average (EMA) are two popular forms, with the latter giving more weight to recent prices.

- *Relative Strength Index (RSI)*: A momentum oscillator measuring the speed and change of price movements. RSI values range from 0 to 100, with readings above 70 typically indicating overbought conditions and readings below 30 indicating oversold conditions.

- *Bollinger Bands*: Comprise a moving average and two standard deviation lines, providing a measure of market volatility. When prices move closer to the upper band, the asset is considered overbought, and when it moves closer to the lower band, it is considered oversold.

- *MACD (Moving Average Convergence Divergence)*: Combines two EMAs to show changes in strength, direction, momentum, and duration of a trend. The MACD line crossing above the signal line is typically a buy signal, while crossing below is a sell signal.

Volume Analysis

Volume is a critical component of technical analysis, indicating the number of shares or contracts traded in a security or market during a given period. Analyzing volume alongside price provides deeper insights into the strength of a price movement. For instance, a price increase on high volume suggests strong buying interest and a sustainable uptrend, whereas the same price increase on low volume may signal a lack of conviction and potential reversal.

Volume indicators, such as the On-Balance Volume (OBV) and the Volume Price Trend (VPT), integrate volume data with price changes to provide a more nuanced understanding of market dynamics. OBV, for example, adds volume on up days and subtracts volume on down days, to measure cumulative buying and selling pressure.

Support and Resistance Levels

Support and resistance levels are horizontal lines used to denote price points at which an asset tends to stop and reverse direction. Support levels represent the price at which an asset finds buying interest strong enough to prevent the price from falling further. Conversely, resistance levels represent the price at which selling interest is sufficiently strong to prevent the price from rising further.

These levels are critical in price formation, as they often correspond to significant psychological barriers or historical price points where considerable trading activity has occurred. Traders watch these levels closely, as breaches of support or resistance can indicate potential breaks in trends and significant opportunities for trading actions.

Trend Analysis

Identifying and analyzing trends is a foundational aspect of technical analysis. Trends can be upward (bullish), downward (bearish), or sideways (consolidation), and recognizing the currently dominant trend is crucial for making informed trading decisions. Techniques such as drawing trendlines, which connect successive lows in an uptrend or successive highs in a downtrend, are instrumental In clarifying the underlying price direction.

Furthermore, trends are often considered in the context of multiple time horizons, including short-term, intermediate-term, and long-term perspectives. Aligning trading strategies with the primary trend across these timeframes can enhance the probability of profitable trades.

Through a combination of price chart patterns, technical indicators, volume analysis, and trend identification, technical analysis offers a comprehensive framework for understanding and predicting price behavior in financial markets. Mastering these techniques empowers traders and investors to make more informed decisions, leveraging the cyclicality of market movements to capture gains and manage risks effectively.

3.5   Impact of News and Events

In the dynamic environment of financial markets, news and events exert a profound influence on price discovery and formation. Traders and investors alike must understand how and why these external factors can lead to rapid and often unpredictable price movements. This section will explore the various ways in which news and events impact market prices, offering insights into how to navigate these developments strategically.

The immediate reaction of market participants to news can trigger significant price movements. This reaction is often driven by shifts in market sentiment, leading to increased volatility. For instance, the release of economic indicators such as GDP growth rates, employment data, or inflation figures can cause substantial fluctuations in stock prices. Positive indicators often lead to bullish behavior, pushing prices higher, while negative indicators can precipitate bearish trends, resulting in price declines.

Corporate news, including earnings reports, mergers and acquisitions, or changes in executive leadership, also plays a crucial role in shaping market expectations and price movements. For example, an earnings report that exceeds market expectations typically results in a price surge. Conversely, earnings that fall short of expectations can lead to a sell-off. Market participants scrutinize such reports not just for the raw numbers but for guidance on future performance, impacting price formation significantly.

Geopolitical events represent another dimension of market influence. Political instability, military conflicts, and trade negotiations can drastically affect market confidence and price stability. A case in point is the impact of trade negotiations between major economies such as the US and China. Announcements regarding trade agreements or tensions can lead to notable market swings as traders react to the potential economic repercussions.

Market impact from unexpected natural disasters or public health crises also cannot be understated. The COVID-19 pandemic is a prime example where global markets experienced unprecedented turmoil. Rapid dissemination of news regarding the spread of the virus and its economic impacts induced sharp declines in stock prices, necessitating swift adjustments to trading strategies.

To effectively manage the impact of news and events, traders often employ event-driven strategies. These strategies involve taking positions in anticipation of specific announcements or in reaction to news events. An example is the use of algorithmic trading systems designed to respond instantly to news releases, thus exploiting momentary price inefficiencies. Algorithms can parse large volumes of news data, gauge sentiment, and execute trades within milliseconds, often leading to profitable outcomes.

Furthermore, understanding the temporal aspects of news impact is essential. Prices may react sharply immediately following an announcement and then stabilize as the market absorbs and processes the new information. This phenomenon is reflected in the concept of the "news impact curve," which describes the initial spike in volatility followed by a gradual decline. Savvy traders can leverage this pattern, positioning themselves to benefit from both the initial reaction and subsequent stabilization.

However, it is imperative to consider the noise-to-signal ratio in news. Not all news has a substantive impact on asset prices. Traders must develop a keen sense for distinguishing between significant news that can alter market fundamentals and minor events that may generate only fleeting price fluctuations.

Incorporating news analysis and event impact into trading strategies also calls for an understanding of behavioral finance. Market participants' overreactions or under-reactions to news can create opportunities for astute investors. Behavioral biases such as herding, where traders mimic the actions of a larger group, can exaggerate price movements and create advantageous entry or exit points.

Equipping oneself with the tools to monitor news flow effectively is key. Utilizing financial news platforms, subscribing to economic calendars, and staying attuned to real-time news feeds can enhance a trader's ability to anticipate and react to price movements. Incorporating sentiment analysis tools, which evaluate the tone and context of news stories, can also provide a deeper understanding of potential market reactions.

Understanding the multi-faceted impact of news and events on price formation enriches the trader's arsenal, fostering a more informed and strategic approach to navigating the complexities of financial markets.

3.6 Market Sentiment and Behavioral Finance

Understanding market sentiment and behavioral finance is crucial for comprehending the nuances of price discovery in financial markets. Market sentiment refers to the overall attitude of investors toward a particular financial market or asset, which can significantly influence price movements. Behavioral finance, on the other hand, examines the psychological factors that drive investors' decisions, often leading to irrational actions and market anomalies.

Market sentiment is often gauged through various indicators such as investor polls, volatility indexes, and trading volumes. When traders have a bullish sentiment, they expect prices to go up, leading to increased buying pressure. Conversely, bearish sentiment indicates expectations of falling prices, prompting more selling activity. These collective actions can drive prices away from their fundamental values, at least in the short term.

Common indicators used to measure market sentiment include the *Volatility Index (VIX)*, often referred to as the "fear gauge," and the *Put/-Call ratio*, which compares the trading volume of bearish put options to bullish call options. High VIX values generally correlate with increased market fear and potential downturns, while a higher put/call ratio often signals bearish sentiment.

In behavioral finance, several biases commonly affect investor behavior. One well-documented bias is **herding behavior**, where investors follow the actions of others rather than relying on their own analysis. Herding can cause rapid price escalations or severe crashes, as masses of traders buy into rising trends or sell in falling markets. Another significant bias is **overconfidence**, where investors overestimate their knowledge and ability to predict market movements, often leading to excessive trading and risk-taking.

The *Prospect Theory*, developed by Daniel Kahneman and Amos Tversky, provides further insights into investor behavior. This theory posits that people value gains and losses differently, leading to risk-averse behavior in the face of potential gains and risk-seeking actions when confronted with losses. This can result in phenomena such as the disposition effect, where investors hold on to losing stocks for too long and sell winning stocks too early, contrary to rational investment strategies.

Emotions like fear and greed play a pivotal role in driving market sentiment. Fear can cause panic selling, while greed can lead to asset bubbles as investors rush to buy into rising markets, often ignoring fundamental values. These emotional responses can create significant price volatility, complicating the price discovery process.

Behavioral finance also examines how psychological mechanisms can lead to systematic errors in judgment. **Anchoring** is one such mechanism, where investors overly rely on initial information or specific reference points, affecting their decision-making. For example, an investor might stick to an original purchase price as a benchmark for selling, even when market conditions have changed.

Another notable concept is **mental accounting**, where individuals compartmentalize money into different categories based on subjective criteria. This can lead to irrational decisions, such as treating dividends as income rather than a return on investment, thereby influencing spending and investment choices.

It's also important to consider the impact of **confirmation bias**, where investors favor information that confirms their preconceptions while disregarding contradictory evidence. This bias can lead to overconfidence and poor decision-making, as traders may become blind to risks and market shifts that contradict their initial thesis.

Cognitive biases and market sentiment contribute to the formation of market anomalies and inefficiencies. Recognizing these patterns provides savvy traders with opportunities to capitalize on irrational market behaviors. For example, contrarian investors deliberately take positions against prevailing market sentiment, buying undervalued assets during times of widespread pessimism and selling overvalued assets during periods of excessive optimism.

Yet, leveraging market sentiment and behavioral biases requires cautious navigation. Overestimating one's ability to predict these irrational behaviors can lead to significant losses. Hence, combining sentiment analysis with robust fundamental and technical analysis ensures a more balanced approach.

Understanding market sentiment and behavioral finance not only enriches one's investment strategy but also enhances the ability to interpret market signals more accurately. By acknowledging both the rational and irrational drivers of market movements, investors can make more informed decisions and better anticipate price fluctuations. As the next section on the Efficient Market Hypothesis (EMH) will explore, the extent to which markets reflect all available information and behave efficiently remains a subject of significant debate, further highlighting the intricate dance between rational analysis and behavioral influences in the realm of price discovery.

3.7 Efficient Market Hypothesis and Price Discovery

The Efficient Market Hypothesis (EMH) is a central tenet in modern financial theory that posits financial markets are "informationally efficient." This implies that asset prices fully reflect all available information at any point in time. Understanding the EMH is crucial for grasping how price discovery functions within financial markets, as it challenges the ability of traders to consistently achieve returns that outperform the market.

The EMH can be examined through its three forms: weak, semi-strong, and strong. Each form varies based on the type of information considered in pricing assets.

The weakest form of EMH asserts that current prices reflect all past market data such as historical prices and volumes. The implication here is that no patterns derived from past trading activities can be used to beat the market through technical analysis. Mathematically, this can be represented by a random walk model where price changes are uncorrelated and largely unpredictable.

$$P_t = P_{t-1} + \epsilon_t$$

where ϵ_t is a random error term.

The semi-strong form extends this idea by suggesting that prices not only reflect past market data but also all publicly available information, including financial statements, news releases, and macroeconomic data. Under this form, neither technical analysis nor fundamental analysis can consistently lead to excess returns, since any new information is rapidly incorporated into asset prices.

Finally, the strong form of EMH posits that prices fully reflect all information, both public and private (insider information). This implies an extreme level of market efficiency where even insiders with privileged information cannot consistently achieve higher returns.

The implications of the EMH on price discovery are profound. If markets are indeed efficient in any of these forms, mispricings of assets should be non-existent or extremely rare. This would mean that market prices are the best estimate of an asset's intrinsic value at any given time. However, empirical evidence on market efficiency reveals a more nuanced reality.

Several studies have provided evidence both supporting and challenging the EMH. For instance, anomalies such as the momentum effect, where stocks that have performed well in the past continue to perform well in the future, and the value effect, where stocks with low price-to-earnings ratios tend to outperform, suggest that markets might not be fully efficient. Behavioral finance further complicates this picture by introducing psychological biases such as overconfidence and herd behavior, which can lead to irrational price movements and deviations from the intrinsic value.

Given these insights, traders and investors must adopt a pragmatic approach to market efficiency. While the EMH provides a useful framework for understanding price discovery, it's crucial to recognize that real-world markets may occasionally deviate from the idealized model due to various inefficiencies.

In practical terms, adhering to the principle that "prices reflect all available information" can guide investors in making informed decisions. For instance, knowing that new information is rapidly priced in can minimize the temptation to frantically trade on news releases. Instead, it encourages a more disciplined investment strategy that focuses on long-term value rather than short-term gains.

However, the acknowledgment of market anomalies and behavioral biases suggests that there may be opportunities for astute investors to exploit inefficiencies. This necessitates a balance between believing in market efficiency and being vigilant for instances where markets deviate from this theoretical baseline.

Considering the role of EMH in price discovery, it bridges firmly with the understanding that market prices, while often efficient, are still influenced by an array of factors from historical data and public information to psychological factors. Recognizing the complexity and multi-faceted nature of markets prepares investors to engage more meaningfully in the process of interpreting and acting on price signals.

Thus, the Efficient Market Hypothesis serves not merely as an academic concept but as a practical guide that, though sometimes imperfect, illuminates the inherent challenges and potential strategies in the dynamic arena of financial trading and investing. Understanding the interplay between EMH and real-world market behavior is foundational to mastering the art and science of price discovery.

Chapter 4

Liquidity and Trading Costs

This chapter explores the concept of liquidity, defining it and detailing the methods used to measure it in financial markets. It examines the factors that influence liquidity levels and distinguishes between liquidity providers and takers. The chapter also addresses various trading costs, both explicit and implicit, including the bid-ask spread and its components. Additionally, it discusses how market conditions can impact both liquidity and trading costs, underlining their importance in trading strategy and market functioning.

4.1 Defining Liquidity

Liquidity is a fundamental concept in financial markets that refers to the ability to quickly buy or sell an asset without causing a significant impact on its price. In essence, a liquid market is one where participants can transact swiftly and with minimal price deviation from the asset's fair value. Understanding liquidity is essential for traders and investors as it directly influences execution efficiency, market stability, and overall trading costs.

To comprehend liquidity fully, one must recognize that it encompasses multiple dimensions: depth, breadth, immediacy, and resiliency. Each of these aspects contributes to the overall liquidity of a market and impacts the ease with which trades can be executed.

First and foremost, depth refers to the volume of orders available at the best bid and ask prices. A market is considered deep if there is substantial volume either willing to be bought at the bid price or sold at the ask price. Depth ensures that substantial trades can be executed without substantially moving the price. Mathematically, depth can be quantified by summing the order book's bid and ask volumes.

$$\text{Depth} = \sum(\text{Bid Volume}) + \sum(\text{Ask Volume})$$

Breadth, on the other hand, relates to the market's capacity to handle large transactions without substantial changes in price. A broad market features numerous price levels with considerable volumes at each level. This characteristic helps mitigate the price impact of larger orders, contributing to a market's overall stability.

Immediacy denotes the speed at which transactions can be executed. Markets with high immediacy allow trades to be completed quickly, thus reducing the waiting time for execution. This characteristic is vital for traders who rely on timely transactions to seize market opportunities or manage risk effectively.

Lastly, resiliency is the market's ability to recover from temporary price changes. A resilient market can swiftly revert to its equilibrium price after a large trade. This aspect of liquidity is critical for maintaining a fair and orderly market, as it ensures that temporary imbalances do not lead to prolonged inefficiencies.

To illustrate these dimensions, consider a scenario where a trader attempts to sell a significant quantity of shares in a single transaction. In a liquid market, this order would likely encounter deep and broad order books, facilitating quick execution with minimal price impact. Conversely, an illiquid market might exhibit thin order books and significant price moves, making it difficult to execute the trade efficiently and potentially at a worse price.

Beyond these dimensions, several attributes can further define liquidity. These include trading volume, turnover ratio, and the bid-ask spread. Trading volume indicates the number of shares or contracts traded within a specific period and serves as a direct measure of market activity. Higher trading volumes generally signify greater liquidity, as they reflect active buyer and seller participation.

The turnover ratio, computed as the trading volume divided by the total number of outstanding shares, provides a further perspective on liquidity by indicating how frequently assets within the market change hands.

$$\text{Turnover Ratio} = \frac{\text{Trading Volume}}{\text{Total Outstanding Shares}}$$

Lastly, the bid-ask spread represents the difference between the best bid and ask prices. It is a crucial indicator of the cost to trade an asset and inherently reflects market liquidity. Narrow spreads usually denote higher liquidity, as market participants are willing to trade at prices closer to each other, whereas wider spreads suggest lower liquidity and higher trading costs.

The concept of liquidity is not static; it can vary based on market conditions, time of day, economic events, and other external factors. For instance, liquidity might be abundant during regular trading hours but diminish substantially outside of these periods, such as in after-hours trading sessions. Furthermore, liquidity tends to decline during high volatility periods, such as economic announcements or geopolitical events, as participants become more cautious and widen their bid-ask spreads, thus increasing the cost of trading.

Recognizing and understanding the multifaceted nature of liquidity is paramount for any trader or investor. It drives decision-making processes, risk management strategies, and overall market participation. Appreciation of its nuances allows market participants to navigate trading environments effectively and to minimize adverse impacts on execution and costs. As we delve deeper into the subsequent sections, the interplay between liquidity and trading costs will become more apparent, reinforcing its vital role in the mechanics of trading.

4.2 Measuring Liquidity

Liquidity, a fundamental attribute of financial markets, reflects the ease with which assets can be traded without causing significant price changes. Measuring liquidity accurately is crucial for traders and investors to manage risk and optimize their trading strategies. Several metrics and approaches have been developed to quantify liquidity, each providing unique insights into how liquid a market or asset is.

One of the most straightforward yet powerful ways to measure liquidity is through the *bid-ask spread*. The bid-ask spread represents the difference between the highest price a buyer is willing to pay (bid) and the lowest price a seller is willing to accept (ask). A narrower spread indicates higher liquidity, as there is a smaller gap between the prices at which buyers and sellers are prepared to trade. Mathematically, the bid-ask spread can be expressed as:

$$\text{Bid-Ask Spread} = \text{Ask Price} - \text{Bid Price}$$

The bid-ask spread serves as a primary indicator of liquidity; however, it does not capture the full picture, especially in markets where prices can change rapidly with large orders.

Another important measure is *market depth*, which provides a more comprehensive view of liquidity by considering the volume of buy and sell orders at various price levels. Market depth is often visualized using a depth chart, showing the cumulative volumes of orders on the bid and ask sides of the order book. The greater the market depth, the more liquid the market, as substantial volumes can be traded without causing large price swings.

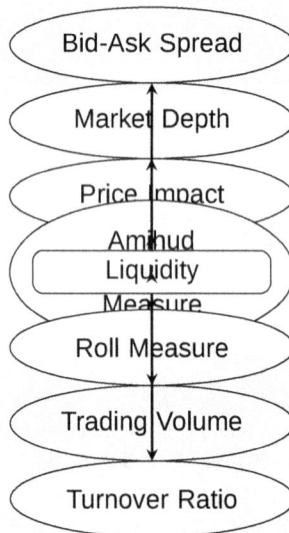

Bid-Ask Spread

Market Depth

Price Impact

Amihud Liquidity Measure

Roll Measure

Trading Volume

Turnover Ratio

Liquidity Measures

Additionally, the concept of *price impact* is crucial in understanding liquidity. Price impact refers to the change in an asset's price caused by a particular trade size. High liquidity markets tend to have lower price impacts for substantial trades. The marginal price impact of a trade can be estimated by analyzing how prices change in response to varying trade volumes.

$$\text{Price Impact} = \frac{\Delta P}{\Delta Q}$$

where ΔP is the change in price and ΔQ is the change in quantity traded. This relationship reveals how sensitive the market price is to trade sizes, providing insights into liquidity conditions.

To further measure liquidity, one can consider the *Amihud Illiquidity Ratio*, introduced by Yakov Amihud. This ratio helps to quantify the daily price response associated with one dollar of trading volume and is calculated as:

$$\text{Amihud Illiquidity Ratio (ILLIQ)} = \frac{1}{N} \sum_{t=1}^{N} \frac{|R_t|}{V_t}$$

where R_t is the return on day t, V_t is the dollar trading volume on day t, and N is the number of observations. A higher value of the Amihud ratio indicates lower liquidity, as it suggests a greater price movement relative to the trading volume.

Another subtle but insightful liquidity measure is the *Roll measure*, named after Richard Roll. The Roll measure utilizes the covariance of consecutive price changes to infer the bid-ask spread, assuming that the presence of a bid-ask bounce (fluctuations between bid and ask prices) is a dominant feature in the price movements:

$$\text{Roll Measure} = 2\sqrt{-\text{Cov}(P_t, P_{t-1})}$$

where P_t and P_{t-1} are consecutive transaction prices. Negative covariance between successive price changes generally indicates that trades oscillate between bid and ask prices, allowing the Roll measure to estimate the effective spread for that asset.

Liquidity can also be evaluated using *trading volume* and *turnover ratio*. Trading volume represents the amount of an asset traded over a given period and serves as a direct indicator of liquidity—higher volumes typically indicate higher liquidity. The turnover ratio, defined as the ratio of trading volume to the number of shares outstanding, offers additional insights by normalizing volume relative to the size of the asset's float.

$$\text{Turnover Ratio} = \frac{\text{Trading Volume}}{\text{Shares Outstanding}}$$

Integrating these various measures provides a holistic understanding of liquidity. While no single metric can capture all dimensions of liquidity, a combination of bid-ask spreads, market depth, price impact, Amihud Illiquidity Ratio, Roll measure, trading volume, and turnover ratios collectively offers a robust framework to assess liquidity conditions in financial markets. These measures are invaluable for traders and investors, enabling them to navigate the complexities of market structure and execution with greater precision and confidence.

4.3   Factors Affecting Liquidity

Liquidity is a multifaceted aspect of financial markets, influenced by a variety of factors that can vary over time and across different market conditions. Understanding these factors is crucial for traders and investors as they navigate the complexities of buying and selling assets efficiently. This section delves into the primary elements that affect liquidity, emphasizing their interconnected nature and the implications for market participants.

One of the most significant factors impacting liquidity is **market depth**. Market depth refers to the volume of buy and sell orders at various price levels in a financial market. When market depth is substantial, it indicates a large number of orders tightly clustered around the current market price, which facilitates smoother and more efficient trading. Conversely, shallow market depth can lead to significant price swings and difficulty executing large trades without causing notable price distortions. The resilience of a market to absorb large orders without substantial price impact is indicative of its depth and overall liquidity.

Another crucial determinant of liquidity is **trading volume**, which reflects the number of shares or contracts traded within a specific time frame. High trading volume signals active market participation and is generally associated with greater liquidity. With more active traders, there are more opportunities to match buy and sell orders quickly, reducing the likelihood of price slippage. Markets with consistently high trading volumes, such as those for major equity indices or heavily traded commodities, tend to offer better liquidity conditions compared to thinly traded markets.

The presence and behavior of **market makers** and **liquidity providers** also play a pivotal role in determining liquidity levels. Market makers are entities or individuals who commit to buying and selling securities to provide continuous bid and ask quotes, thus ensuring market stability and liquidity. By standing ready to trade, market makers reduce the time it takes to match buyers with sellers, thereby enhancing the market's overall liquidity. Their profitability, which relies on earning the bid-ask spread, incentivizes them to manage inventory and mitigate risks, ultimately affecting how tight or wide spreads are in the market.

Information asymmetry among market participants can also dramatically impact liquidity. When certain participants possess superior information, it can lead to a situation where informed traders quickly act on their knowledge, leaving less-informed traders hesitant to trade, fearing adverse selection. This dynamic can cause a decrease in overall trading activity and widen bid-ask spreads, diminishing liquidity. Efforts to reduce information asymmetry, such as through enhanced disclosure and transparency regulations, are essential in maintaining a more liquid market environment.

Regulatory frameworks and **market structure** are additional influences on liquidity. Regulations that promote transparency, fair trading practices, and competition among market participants tend to enhance liquidity. For instance, rules that limit price manipulation and promote market integrity encourage investor confidence, which can lead to increased trading activity and liquidity. Moreover, the design of trading venues—whether they are order-driven or quote-driven markets, electronic or floor-based exchanges—can affect how efficiently buy and sell orders are matched, further impacting liquidity.

Macroeconomic factors and broader market conditions cannot be overlooked when considering liquidity. Economic indicators such as interest rates, inflation rates, and overall economic growth play a significant role. During periods of economic stability and growth, investor confidence tends to be higher, leading to increased trading volumes and enhanced liquidity. Conversely, during economic downturns or periods of high uncertainty, even traditionally liquid markets can experience reduced trading activity and higher volatility, thus impacting liquidity.

Technological advancements, particularly in the realm of algorithmic and high-frequency trading (HFT), have had a profound effect on market liquidity. Algorithmic trading, through its use of sophisticated software to execute trades at high speed and frequency, can both provide and consume liquidity. While market-making algorithms can enhance liquidity by offering tighter spreads, aggressive HFT strategies can sometimes lead to liquidity withdrawal, particularly in highly volatile conditions. Understanding these dual roles is essential for market participants assessing liquidity.

Finally, **investor behavior and sentiment** are fundamental to liquidity. Behavioral factors, such as herd behavior, contrarian strategies, and panic selling, can significantly influence market liquidity. For instance, in times of market stress, a widespread move to liquidate positions can exacerbate market declines, reducing liquidity as buyers become scarce. On the other hand, periods of optimism and bullish sentiment generally coincide with higher trading volumes and better liquidity conditions.

Understanding the intricate interplay of these factors provides traders and investors with the knowledge to navigate varying liquidity conditions effectively. By recognizing the underlying causes of liquidity fluctuations, market participants can better manage their trading costs, optimize their execution strategies, and achieve more favorable outcomes in their trading activities.

4.4 Liquidity Providers and Takers

In exploring the dynamic landscape of market liquidity, it is essential to understand the roles of liquidity providers and liquidity takers. These two types of market participants play a fundamental role in the functioning of financial markets, influencing not only the availability of liquidity but also the efficiency and stability of trading activities.

Liquidity providers are entities or individuals who supply liquidity to the market by posting buy and sell orders. They are often referred to as market makers because they create a market within the order book, providing other participants with the opportunity to execute trades. These participants often profit from the bid-ask spread, which is the difference between the higher price at which they can sell (ask price) and the lower price at which they can buy (bid price). By continuously offering to buy and sell securities, liquidity providers facilitate smoother trading and contribute to market depth and resilience.

Market makers typically use sophisticated algorithms to manage their inventory and minimize risk. These algorithms evaluate the current market conditions, historical data, and other relevant factors to set optimal bid and ask prices. For instance, a simple quote-driven market-making strategy might involve placing limit orders at predefined distances from the market price to capture the bid-ask spread profit while dynamically adjusting based on market fluctuations. This continuous adjustment helps in maintaining equilibrium in the market.

$$P_{bid} = P_{mid} - \delta, \quad P_{ask} = P_{mid} + \delta$$

where P_{bid} is the bid price, P_{ask} is the ask price, P_{mid} is the mid-point price, and δ is the spread adjustment factor.

On the other hand, liquidity takers are the participants who execute trades by accepting the prices set by liquidity providers. These trades are typically market orders, which are executed immediately at the best available prices. Liquidity takers are often institutional investors, hedge funds, or individual traders who need to execute a trade quickly and are willing to incur the cost of the bid-ask spread to do so. Their motivation can range from taking advantage of market inefficiencies, reducing exposure to risk, or leveraging time-sensitive market opportunities.

While liquidity providers and takers perform distinct roles, their interaction is crucial for the functioning of financial markets. The presence of active liquidity providers can reduce transaction costs for liquidity takers, fostering an environment where prices reflect true market sentiment more accurately. Conversely, a high volume of liquidity takers can prompt liquidity providers to widen their spreads to hedge against the increasing risk of adverse price movements.

A critical aspect of the relationship between these participants is the concept of adverse selection. Liquidity providers face the risk that liquidity takers possess superior information about future price movements, leading the provider to trade at unfavorable prices. To mitigate this risk, liquidity providers may adjust their spreads dynamically, making them wider in times of high uncertainty or market stress.

Empirical evidence suggests that the interaction between liquidity providers and takers significantly impacts market efficiency and liquidity levels. For instance, studies have shown that markets with a higher prevalence of algorithmic traders, who often act as liquidity providers, tend to have lower spreads and higher market depth. This is attributable to the algorithms' ability to quickly process and respond to new information, maintaining continuous market activity.

Moreover, regulatory frameworks often influence the behavior of liquidity providers and takers. Market regulations designed to ensure fairness and transparency can affect the strategies employed by these participants. For example, restrictions on high-frequency trading or the implementation of minimum tick sizes can modify the profitability of market-making strategies, thereby impacting the overall liquidity in the market.

Understanding the roles and interplay of liquidity providers and takers equips traders and investors with the knowledge to navigate market intricacies more effectively. By recognizing the significance of their interactions, market participants can better comprehend the sources of liquidity, anticipate changes in trading conditions, and develop strategies that align with their investment goals.

In the evolving landscape of financial markets, the delicate balance between liquidity providers and takers continues to be a pivotal element in maintaining market integrity and functionality. Enhancing our understanding of this interplay offers valuable insights into the mechanics driving market behavior, ultimately empowering traders and investors to make informed and strategic decisions.

4.5   Trading Costs: Explicit and Implicit

Understanding trading costs is crucial for developing a successful trading strategy as these costs directly affect the net returns of any trade. Trading costs can be broadly divided into two categories: explicit and implicit costs. Grasping the distinction between these two types can help traders optimize their strategies and manage their portfolios more efficiently.

Explicit costs are the out-of-pocket expenses directly associated with executing a trade. These include brokerage commissions, exchange fees, and taxes. Brokerage commissions are fees charged by brokers for facilitating trades. These can vary significantly depending on the broker, the trading platform, and the volume of trading. For example, traditional brokerage houses might charge a higher commission compared to discount brokers. Additionally, some brokers might offer tiered pricing based on the volume of trades executed, which can be benefi-

68

cial for high-frequency traders.

Exchange fees are charges levied by stock exchanges for the execution of trades on their platforms. These fees can differ based on the exchange and the type of financial instrument being traded. Taxes, such as capital gains tax or transaction tax, also fall under explicit costs. These taxes can vary by country and can have a substantial impact on the net returns from trading activities.

Implicit costs, on the other hand, are less visible and often harder to quantify but are equally important. These include the bid-ask spread, market impact costs, and opportunity costs. The bid-ask spread is the difference between the highest price a buyer is willing to pay (bid) and the lowest price a seller is willing to accept (ask). This spread can be influenced by liquidity levels, market volatility, and the specific asset being traded. A wider spread generally indicates higher implicit costs and vice versa.

Market impact costs occur when the act of executing a large order moves the market price against the trader. For example, a large buy order might drive the price up before the order is fully executed, resulting in the trader buying at higher prices than initially intended. This is particularly relevant for institutional traders dealing with large volumes. To minimize market impact costs, traders often employ strategies such as breaking large orders into smaller batches or utilizing algorithmic trading techniques that execute orders gradually over time.

Opportunity costs represent the potential gains that could have been achieved had the capital been deployed differently. For instance, if a trader purchases a stock and it depreciates in value, the opportunity cost is the return that could have been earned if the capital was invested in a different asset that performed better. Opportunity costs emphasize the importance of strategic asset allocation and the necessity of periodic portfolio review and rebalancing.

To illustrate these concepts mathematically, consider a trade where a trader buys 100 shares of a stock with the following parameters:

- Purchase price: $50 per share

- Brokerage commission: $10

- Bid-ask spread: $0.05 per share (spread is usually quoted as cents per share)

- Market impact: estimated at $0.02 per share

The total explicit cost of this trade would be the brokerage commission:

$$\text{Explicit Cost} = \$10$$

For implicit costs, the calculation involves both the bid-ask spread and market impact:

$$\text{Bid-Ask Spread Cost} = 100 \text{ shares} \times \$0.05 = \$5$$

$$\text{Market Impact Cost} = 100 \text{ shares} \times \$0.02 = \$2$$

Therefore, the total implicit cost is:

$$\text{Implicit Cost} = \$5 + \$2 = \$7$$

Combining both explicit and implicit costs, the total cost of the trade becomes:
$$\text{Total Trading Cost} = \$10 + \$7 = \$17$$

These calculations demonstrate how explicit and implicit costs accumulate to affect overall trading expenses. By understanding and minimizing these costs, traders can enhance the efficiency and profitability of their trading activities.

Without acknowledging these costs, traders might find their expected returns significantly diminished. Integrating this knowledge into a trading strategy involves diligent planning, selecting cost-effective brokers, employing market-aware order execution strategies, and continuously monitoring market conditions for signs of increased volatility or widening spreads that could escalate trading costs. In today's competitive and technologically advanced marketplace, being vigilant about both explicit and implicit costs is essential for sustaining a profitable trading career.

4.6   Bid-Ask Spread and Its Components

The bid-ask spread is a fundamental concept in financial markets, acting as both a measure of market liquidity and a cost of trading. This section aims to provide a comprehensive understanding of the bid-ask spread, delving into its components and the various factors that influence its width. By the end of this section, readers should have a nuanced appreciation of how the bid-ask spread affects their trading decisions and overall market dynamics.

The bid-ask spread is defined as the difference between the highest price a buyer is willing to pay for an asset (the bid) and the lowest price a seller is willing to accept (the ask). Mathematically, it is expressed as:

$$\text{Bid-Ask Spread} = \text{Ask Price} - \text{Bid Price}$$

To illustrate this with a simple example, consider a stock with a current bid price of $100 and an ask price of $102. The bid-ask spread in this case would be $2. This spread represents the transaction cost for market participants, effectively imposing a barrier to immediate, cost-free trading.

The bid-ask spread can be broken down into several components, each influenced by different market factors. These components include:

- **Order Processing Costs:** This element of the spread arises from the fundamental expenses incurred by market makers or liquidity providers in the process of executing and clearing trades. These costs encompass the technology required for fast and efficient trade execution, the salaries of the personnel managing the trades, and the overheads involved in maintaining a trading desk. While individually small, these costs accumulate and must be covered by the spread to ensure the financial viability of market making activities.

- **Inventory Risk:** Market makers often hold inventories of the securities they trade, exposing them to price fluctuations that can result In losses. The inventory risk component of the bid-ask spread compensates them for the potential adverse price movements while they hold these securities. For instance, if a market maker buys a stock at the bid price, they incur the risk that the price may decline before they can resell it at the ask price. This risk is particularly pronounced in volatile markets, where rapid price movements are more likely.

- **Adverse Selection:** Adverse selection occurs when one party in a transaction has more or better information than the other. In the context of financial markets, this typically means that the counterparties to market makers might possess superior knowledge about an asset's value. To protect themselves from trading against better-informed investors, market makers widen the spread. This compensates for the likelihood that they may transact at unfavorable prices. For example, if a seller is well-informed about negative news not yet reflected in the asset price, they may sell at the ask price, leaving the market maker vulnerable to a subsequent price drop.

- **Liquidity Premium:** The final component of the bid-ask spread is the liquidity premium. This reflects the compensation required by market makers for providing liquidity in less liquid markets. In such markets, finding a counterpart for a trade can be more challenging, and the cost of holding inventory for longer periods is higher. Therefore, market makers demand a premium, reflected in a wider spread, to compensate for these additional risks and costs. In highly liquid markets, this premium is lower, resulting in narrower spreads.

Several factors influence the width of the bid-ask spread:

- **Trading Volume:** Higher trading volumes generally lead to narrower spreads as the high frequency of transactions reduces both inventory risk and the liquidity premium.

- **Price Volatility:** Increased price volatility tends to widen spreads, reflecting the higher inventory risk and potential adverse selection faced by market makers.

- **Market Competition:** More intense competition among market makers usually results in narrower spreads, as firms vie for trading flows by offering more competitive pricing.

- **Information Asymmetry:** Greater disparities in information between market participants widen spreads as market makers seek to protect themselves from adverse selection.

Understanding the components and determinants of the bid-ask spread is crucial for traders and investors. A narrower spread reduces transaction costs and enhances trading efficiency, while a wider spread signifies higher trading costs and potential risks. As market conditions fluctuate, being cognizant of these changes and their impact on the bid-ask spread can aid in optimizing trading strategies and managing costs effectively.

This deep dive into the mechanics of the bid-ask spread underscores its critical role in market functioning. Whether you are executing trades or providing liquidity, recognizing the factors at play can significantly inform your approach to the financial markets.

4.7   Impact of Market Conditions on Liquidity and Costs

Market conditions play a pivotal role in shaping both liquidity and trading costs in financial markets. Understanding these dynamics is crucial for traders and investors, as market conditions can vary significantly across different time frames and market states. This section delves into the intricate ways through which market conditions influence liquidity levels and the associated trading costs. By examining these relationships, we can better anticipate market behavior and optimize our trading strategies.

One of the fundamental aspects to consider is the market's overall volatility. High volatility often leads to wider bid-ask spreads, as market makers demand greater compensation for the increased risk. During periods of heightened volatility, liquidity can become fragmented, resulting in less depth at each price level. Conversely, in stable and low-volatility environments, bid-ask spreads tend to narrow, and market depth improves, facilitating smoother and more cost-effective trading.

In addition to volatility, economic events and news releases are powerful catalysts impacting liquidity and trading costs. Major announcements, such as central bank interest rate decisions, employment reports, or geopolitical developments, can lead to abrupt changes in market sentiment. Traders keen on navigating these events must account for the potential for rapid liquidity erosion and spike in transaction costs. For instance, during a major economic release, the sudden influx of orders can overwhelm market makers, temporarily widening spreads and impacting the executable prices.

The state of order flow also bears significant weight on liquidity. An imbalance between buy and sell orders can create liquidity shortages and increased costs. A heavy skew towards buying interest might deplete the available liquidity on the offer side, driving prices up and leading to greater slippage for large orders. Conversely, a predominance of selling can push prices down sharply, exacerbating impact costs. Efficient order execution strategies, such as slicing large orders into smaller increments or using algorithmic trading techniques, can help mitigate these effects by optimizing the timing and manner of order placement.

Another critical factor is the market's structural environment. The presence of high-frequency trading (HFT) firms, dark pools, and other non-transparent venues can both add to and subtract from visible liquidity. HFT firms often provide substantial liquidity during normal conditions but may withdraw swiftly during turbulent periods, creating sudden liquidity vacuums. Dark pools, while providing anonymity, can divert order flow away from public exchanges, affecting the observable volume and depth. Traders need to be adept at navigating across various trading venues to capture the best available liquidity and minimize costs.

Market microstructure elements such as tick size, lot sizes, and trading hours similarly influence liquidity conditions. A smaller tick size, for example, can enhance liquidity by narrowing spreads and increasing the number of price levels available for trading. However, it may also lead to higher price competition among liquidity providers, influencing their willingness to post orders. Extended trading hours, while offering greater flexibility, often come with reduced liquidity outside of primary market times. Understanding these nuances helps in planning trades to ensure optimal liquidity and lower execution costs.

Behavioral aspects of market participants also shape liquidity and costs. Herding behavior, where traders collectively follow the same trend, can amplify market movements and create temporary liquidity shortages. Periods of panic selling or exuberant buying often result in significant deviations from fundamental values, impacting liquidity and execution prices. Recognizing these patterns allows traders to anticipate potential liquidity crunches and adapt their strategies accordingly.

Finally, regulatory changes and market interventions by authorities can have profound and sometimes rapid effects on liquidity conditions. New regulations around short selling, circuit breakers, or transaction taxes can alter trading behaviors and liquidity provision. Market interventions, such as central bank policies or government measures during crises, often aim to stabilize markets but can also introduce temporary distortions in normal trading conditions.

By carefully analyzing the interplay between market conditions and liquidity dynamics, traders can better align their strategies to effectively manage risks and control costs. Staying aware of volatility trends, major economic events, order flow imbalances, microstructure specifics, participant behaviors, and regulatory landscape is essential in making informed trading decisions that enhance profitability while mitigating adverse impacts on liquidity and costs.

Chapter 5

The Role of Market Makers

This chapter investigates the critical role of market makers in financial markets, detailing their functions and the strategies they employ to provide liquidity and facilitate trading. It explores how market makers enhance market efficiency by narrowing bid-ask spreads and ensuring smoother transaction flows. The chapter also outlines the risks market makers face, such as inventory risk and adverse selection, and examines their operations within different market structures. Additionally, it covers the regulatory frameworks governing market makers, emphasizing their importance in maintaining market stability and integrity.

5.1   Who Are Market Makers?

Market makers are pivotal entities in financial markets, playing a crucial role in ensuring liquidity and efficient trading. At their core, market makers are firms or individuals tasked with the responsibility of continuously providing buy and sell quotes for a given security, thereby facilitating trading and contributing to market fluidity.

Market makers operate by posting both bid (the price at which they are willing to buy) and ask (the price at which they are willing to sell) prices for a security. The difference between these two prices is known as the bid-ask spread, which represents the profit margin for the market maker, assuming they are able to buy at the bid price and sell at the ask price. By maintaining this spread, market makers are able to earn a relatively consistent profit, provided they manage their inventories effectively and mitigate risks.

To illustrate the function of a market maker in more detail, consider the following example involving a hypothetical stock, ABC Corp. Suppose the current market environment reflects a bid price of $100 and an ask price of $102 for ABC Corp. The market maker would stand ready to purchase shares from sellers at $100 and sell shares to buyers at $102, profiting from the $2 spread. This continuous quoting behavior ensures that there is always a counterparty available for traders wishing to either buy or sell ABC Corp's stock.

Market makers are often intermediaries such as brokerage firms, investment banks, or specialized trading firms. These entities utilize sophisticated technology and algorithms to manage their quoting activity efficiently and to minimize the risk inherent in holding large inventories of securities. The use of algorithmic trading allows market makers to swiftly update their quotes in response to market conditions, ensuring tight spreads and high liquidity.

One essential characteristic of market makers is their dual role as both buyers and sellers. This commitment requires significant capital resources since they need to be capable of fulfilling large orders without creating substantial market impact. To manage this aspect, market makers typically employ risk management strategies, including delta hedging, which aims to offset the risk associated with their inventory holdings through derivatives or other financial instruments.

Market makers are particularly important in markets with less intrinsic liquidity. For example, in over-the-counter (OTC) markets or in less frequently traded stocks, the presence of market makers is critical to ensuring that investors can execute trades promptly without facing significant price volatility. Without market makers, such markets might suffer from wide bid-ask spreads and low transaction volumes, which could deter investors and undermine market confidence.

The role of market makers is not limited to equities; they are also integral to the functioning of other asset classes, such as fixed income, foreign exchange, and commodities. In each of these markets, market makers adjust their strategies and operations to suit the specific characteristics of the instruments they trade. For instance, in the foreign exchange market, market makers might utilize advanced pricing models that incorporate macroeconomic indicators, interest rate differentials, and geopolitical factors to set competitive quotes.

Beyond mere liquidity provision, market makers contribute to the overall efficiency and stability of financial markets. By narrowing bid-ask spreads, they reduce transaction costs for investors, enhancing price discovery and market depth. Market makers also help mitigate price volatility by absorbing temporary imbalances between supply and demand, which might otherwise lead to sharp and erratic price movements.

To incentivize and regulate the activities of market makers, exchanges and regulatory bodies impose certain obligations and offer benefits. Market makers may be required to adhere to minimum quoting obligations, such as maintaining two-sided quotes for a set percentage of the trading day or within specified price ranges. In return, they might receive rebates or fee reductions from the exchange, recognizing their contribution to market quality.

Understanding who market makers are and the essential role they play provides a foundational insight into the mechanics of modern financial markets. As we progress through this chapter, we will delve deeper into the functions, strategies, and challenges faced by market makers, further illuminating their critical importance in maintaining vibrant and efficient markets.

5.2 Functions of Market Makers

Market makers play a pivotal role in financial markets, serving as intermediaries who facilitate trading by providing liquidity and maintaining efficient market operations. Their presence ensures that traders can consistently buy and sell securities, even in times of market stress. In this section, we delve into the specific functions of market makers, elucidating their crucial contributions to market dynamics.

At the core, market makers stand ready to quote both buy (bid) and sell (ask) prices for a set number of shares, thus offering continuous two-sided markets. This dual quoting system fosters liquidity, as it guarantees that there are always prices available for executing trades. In the absence of market makers, liquidity would be sporadic, and the bid-ask spreads would widen dramatically, increasing transaction costs for all market participants.

Market makers enhance price discovery by actively trading and adjusting their quotes in response to supply and demand forces. As they continuously update their prices to reflect new information, they help in creating a more accurate and timely valuation of the traded securities. This constant price adjustment facilitates market transparency and the efficient dissemination of information.

In addition to quoting prices, market makers absorb temporary imbalances in the market. For instance, if there is an excess of sell orders and insufficient buy orders, market makers will step in to buy the surplus, preventing abrupt price drops and ensuring smoother transitions between buy and sell pressures. By mitigating these imbalances, market makers contribute to market stability and prevent erratic price movements.

Market makers also engage in arbitrage opportunities across different trading venues. They exploit price discrepancies by buying low in one market and selling high in another. Such activities are beneficial to the market as a whole, as they align prices across various exchanges, reducing inefficiencies and promoting a unified market price.

The commitment of market makers extends to providing liquidity during volatile periods. When market stress induces a pullback of liquidity from other traders, market makers uphold their obligation to offer quotations. This resilience ensures continuous trading and aids in calming the market during turbulence, underscoring their importance in maintaining market integrity.

Moreover, market makers serve as essential participants in initial public offerings (IPOs) by stabilizing prices once the stock begins trading. They employ stabilization strategies such as over-allotment options (greenshoe) and aftermarket support to mitigate volatility and support a fair and orderly market for newly listed securities.

The ability of market makers to manage large inventories of securities is another critical function. They maintain a balanced inventory, carefully managing the risk associated with holding significant positions. Effective inventory management helps in sustaining tight bid-ask spreads and providing enhanced liquidity, which are vital for efficient market functioning.

Market makers also interact closely with other market participants, including institutional investors, retail investors, and other traders. Through these interactions, market makers gather proprietary trade information that enables them to better predict market movements and enhance their trading strategies. This knowledge benefits the overall market by fostering informed decision-making and contributing to a more robust trading environment.

Finally, market makers aid in reducing the volatility of lesser-traded or illiquid securities. By prioritizing these securities, they ensure that even stocks with lower trading volumes have sufficient liquidity. This action benefits smaller companies and their investors by providing more consistent trading opportunities, thereby improving market access and fairness.

In essence, the myriad functions of market makers are indispensable for the health and efficiency of financial markets. Their continuous presence and active participation not only provide liquidity and stability but also enhance the overall trading experience for all market participants. As we move forward, understanding these functions more deeply offers insight into the integral role market makers play in our financial ecosystem.

5.3 Market Maker Strategies

Understanding the strategies employed by market makers is crucial to grasping their role in financial markets. These strategies are designed to balance the twin objectives of providing liquidity and managing risk, ensuring that market makers can operate efficiently within the confines of market dynamics.

A core component of market maker strategies is the continuous provision of bid and ask quotes. Market makers strive to maintain a presence on both sides of the order book, quoting prices at which they are willing to buy (bid) and sell (ask) securities. The difference between these two prices is known as the bid-ask spread. A narrower spread indicates a more liquid market and is generally preferred by traders.

Market makers set their bid and ask prices based on several factors, including supply and demand for the security, current market conditions, and their inventory levels. To optimize their quote placements, market makers often employ sophisticated algorithms that analyze market data in real-time. These algorithms can adjust quotes dynamically, ensuring that the market maker's quotes remain competitive while also managing the risk of adverse price movements.

Another key strategy involves inventory management. Since market makers earn profits from the bid-ask spread, maintaining an optimal inventory level is critical. Holding too much inventory exposes the market maker to significant price risk, while holding too little may reduce their ability to provide liquidity and capture spreads. To address this, market makers use various hedging techniques, such as trading correlated securities or using derivatives, to mitigate the risks associated with holding inventory.

Furthermore, market makers may engage in statistical arbitrage. This involves using quantitative models to identify and exploit price inefficiencies between related securities. By simultaneously buying and selling these securities, market makers can lock in low-risk profits. For instance, if a market maker detects that a stock is temporarily overpriced relative to its historical mean, they might short-sell the stock while taking a long position in a related asset, expecting the price misalignment to correct over time.

High-frequency trading (HFT) is another important strategy used by some market makers. HFT relies on extremely fast execution and sophisticated algorithms to capitalize on fleeting market opportunities. These algorithms can execute thousands of trades per second, allowing market makers to rapidly adjust their positions and quotes to capitalize on minute price discrepancies. While HFT can enhance market liquidity, it also requires significant technological infrastructure and bears the risk of amplifying market volatility.

In addition to automated strategies, market makers also rely on human judgment and expertise, particularly during periods of market stress or when trading less-liquid securities. Experienced traders can assess market sentiment, news events, and other qualitative factors that may not be fully captured by algorithms. By leveraging their market intuition, these traders can make informed decisions about quote placements, inventory adjustments, and risk management.

Market makers also participate in dark pools and other alternative trading systems (ATS). These venues allow market makers to execute large orders anonymously, reducing the market impact and potential for adverse price movements. By strategically utilizing dark pools, market makers can manage their inventory and risk exposure more effectively while still providing liquidity to the broader market.

Finally, cooperation with other financial institutions forms a part of market-making strategies. Market makers often establish relationships with institutional investors, brokers, and other market participants to gain insights and access larger pools of liquidity. These relationships can facilitate block trades and allow market makers to better manage large order flows, further enhancing their ability to provide liquidity.

The interplay of these strategies underscores the complexity and sophistication of market makers' operations. By continuously refining their approaches and leveraging technology and expertise, market makers play a vital role in ensuring efficient and stable financial markets. As we delve deeper into the specifics of market makers in different market structures, it becomes clear how these strategies adapt to various trading environments, further highlighting their significance in the broader market ecosystem.

5.4 Market Makers and Liquidity

Liquidity is the lifeblood of any financial market, fundamentally affecting the ease and cost with which assets can be traded. An environment of high liquidity means investors can buy and sell assets quickly without causing significant price changes. Market makers play an indispensable role in ensuring such liquidity, thereby enhancing the overall efficiency of financial markets. This section delves into the intricate relationship between market makers and liquidity, highlighting the mechanisms through which market makers maintain a liquid market.

At the core of their operation, market makers provide liquidity by posting buy (bid) and sell (ask) prices for a given security. By doing so, they stand ready to satisfy the demands of other market participants, whether they are looking to enter or exit positions. For instance, a market maker in stock XYZ might continuously update their quotes as follows:

$$\text{Bid Price} = \$50.00 \quad \text{Ask Price} = \$50.05 \qquad (5.1)$$

In this scenario, the market maker is willing to buy shares from investors at $50.00 and sell them at $50.05. The $0.05 difference, known as the bid-ask spread, represents the market maker's compensation for providing liquidity and bearing various risks.

When a transaction occurs, market makers adjust their positions and quotes dynamically to reflect the latest market conditions. This adjustment process is crucial for maintaining a constant flow of liquidity. For example, if an investor buys 1,000 shares at $50.05, the market maker now holds fewer shares and might update their prices to manage inventory risk:

$$\text{New Bid Price} = \$50.01 \quad \text{New Ask Price} = \$50.10 \quad\quad (5.2)$$

Such adjustments ensure that the market remains balanced and that liquidity is available under various market conditions.

Moreover, market makers often engage in sophisticated algorithmic trading strategies to manage their inventory and handle large order flows effectively. These algorithms are designed to minimize the market impact and ensure that the market maker can continue to offer competitive bid-ask spreads. A common approach involves dynamic hedging, where the market maker uses derivative instruments to offset risks associated with holding large positions in the underlying security.

$$f(x) = \begin{cases} \text{Long Position Hedging} & \text{if } x > 0 \\ \text{Short Position Hedging} & \text{if } x < 0 \\ \text{Neutral} & \text{if } x = 0 \end{cases}$$

In this piecewise function, $f(x)$ represents the hedging strategy based on the position x held by the market maker. By effectively managing these positions, market makers can ensure that their presence in the market has a stabilizing effect, absorbing excess buy and sell orders and thus maintaining liquidity.

Another critical aspect of market makers' contribution to liquidity is their ability to handle significant market stress. During times of volatility, the presence of market makers can prevent drastic price swings by providing consistent quotes, even when market sentiment might discourage other types of traders from participating. Their willingness to take on this role, despite elevated risks, underscores the importance of market makers in preserving orderly and liquid markets.

Additionally, market makers utilize various forms of transaction cost analysis (TCA) to evaluate the effectiveness of their liquidity provision. By constantly analyzing the impact of their trades on market prices, market makers can fine-tune their strategies to minimize market disruption and better serve the market's liquidity needs. TCA involves metrics such as implementation shortfall and market impact cost, which are pivotal in optimizing trading algorithms.

$$\text{Implementation Shortfall} = \frac{\text{Execution Price} - \text{Benchmark Price}}{\text{Benchmark Price}} \times 100\%$$

This formula calculates the percentage deviation of the actual execution price from a pre-determined benchmark price, providing insights into the efficiency of the market maker's liquidity provision.

The symbiotic relationship between market makers and liquidity is bolstered by the incentives provided by exchanges and trading platforms. These incentives often come in the form of rebates or fee structures that reward market makers for their role in maintaining a liquid market. By aligning financial incentives with the provision of liquidity, exchanges ensure that market makers are motivated to perform their functions effectively.

Ultimately, the role of market makers in maintaining liquidity is multi-faceted, involving a delicate balance of posting competitive quotes, managing inventory risk, employing advanced algorithms, and responding dynamically to market conditions. By doing so, they underpin the market's structural integrity, ensuring that assets can be traded efficiently and economically. This robust framework not only facilitates smoother transactions but also boosts investor confidence, fostering a more vibrant and resilient financial market.

5.5   Risks Faced by Market Makers

Market makers play an indispensable role in financial markets by providing liquidity and facilitating trades. However, their operations are not without risks. Understanding these risks is essential for comprehensively appreciating the challenges market makers face and the strategies they employ to mitigate these dangers.

The primary risks faced by market makers can be categorized into inventory risk, adverse selection, and technological risks. Each of these presents unique challenges that require strategic management to ensure the market maker's ongoing profitability and contribution to market efficiency.

- **Inventory risk** arises from the obligation of market makers to buy and sell securities consistently. They continuously manage an inventory of financial instruments, and fluctuations in the market can lead to significant losses. For instance, if a market maker purchases a large volume of a security and the market price subsequently declines, the value of their inventory diminishes, impacting their profitability. To mitigate inventory risk, market makers employ sophisticated hedging techniques, such as using derivatives to offset potential losses in their inventory holdings.

- **Adverse selection** is another critical risk that market makers must navigate. This occurs when market makers deal with traders who have superior information about a financial instrument's true value. In such scenarios, the market maker may be at a disadvantage, buying high from informed sellers or selling low to informed buyers. To combat adverse selection, market makers use advanced algorithmic trading strategies that analyze order flow and attempt to infer the presence of informed traders, adjusting their bid-ask spreads accordingly to protect against potential losses.

- **Technological risks** are increasingly significant in modern financial markets, where trading is dominated by high-frequency and algorithmic trading strategies. Market makers rely on sophisticated technology to execute trades swiftly and efficiently. However, this technology can introduce risks such as system failures, software bugs, and cyber-attacks. Any technological malfunction can lead to significant financial losses and disrupt market operations. Market makers invest heavily in robust technology infrastructure and security measures to minimize these risks, ensuring that their systems are resilient and their trading activities remain uninterrupted.

- Beyond these primary risks, market makers also face regulatory and compliance risks. Financial markets are highly regulated, and market makers must adhere to strict regulatory standards to maintain their licenses and avoid substantial penalties. Compliance with these regulations involves ongoing monitoring and reporting, which can be costly and resource-intensive. However, adherence to regulatory requirements is vital for maintaining market stability and integrity.

In summary, while market makers provide vital services that enhance market liquidity and efficiency, they are constantly exposed to various risks. Effective risk management strategies are crucial for their success and sustainability. Understanding the nature of these risks and the measures taken to mitigate them offers a deeper insight into the complex dynamics of market making and the intricacies of maintaining a balanced and efficient market environment.

5.6 Market Makers in Different Market Structures

Market makers play pivotal roles across various market structures, each of which presents distinct challenges and opportunities. Understanding how market makers operate in these differing environments is essential for appreciating their adaptability and the significant value they bring to the trading landscape.

In centralized exchanges, such as the New York Stock Exchange (NYSE) and NASDAQ, market makers provide consistent liquidity by posting both buy and sell orders on the order book. These exchanges are characterized by their well-defined regulatory frameworks and transparent order matching mechanisms. The central limit order book (CLOB) is a common feature, where trades are executed based on price-time priority. Market makers on these platforms must actively manage their inventories and quote prices to accommodate the high volume of trades while maintaining competitive bid-ask spreads. The use of sophisticated algorithms and real-time data analytics is paramount in these environments, helping market makers make informed decisions and mitigate risks associated with rapid price movements.

Meanwhile, in dealer markets, such as the bond markets or the over-the-counter (OTC) markets, market makers are often large financial institutions acting as dealers. Unlike centralized exchanges, trades in dealer markets usually occur through a network of dealers who quote prices at which they are willing to buy or sell specific securities. These prices may vary between dealers based on their inventory levels, risk exposure, and market views. In this decentralized structure, market makers must build strong client relationships and maintain robust communication channels to facilitate trade negotiations and ensure that liquidity is available even for less liquid securities. The lack of a centralized order book puts greater emphasis on the market makers' ability to source liquidity and manage larger spreads.

Electronic Communication Networks (ECNs), such as Arca and BATS, represent another distinct market structure where market makers operate. ECNs match buy and sell orders through automated platforms, fostering a high-speed trading environment characterized by tight spreads and minimal human intervention. Market makers on ECNs must leverage advanced high-frequency trading (HFT) algorithms to keep pace with the rapid influx of orders and to capitalize on fleeting arbitrage opportunities. Speed and precision are critical, and market makers often co-locate their trading systems near ECN servers to minimize latency. This environment demands investments in cutting-edge technology and continual optimization of trading strategies to remain competitive.

Auction markets, like those of certain commodity exchanges, present a different set of dynamics for market makers. Here, prices are determined through a bidding process where buyers and sellers submit bids and offers, and trades are executed at the highest bid or lowest offer. Market makers in auction markets play a crucial role by standing ready to provide liquidity and by participating in the bidding process to ensure that transactions can occur even when there are no immediate natural counterparties. Their presence helps stabilize prices and reduce the volatility that can arise from sporadic trading activity.

In fragmented markets, where securities trade on multiple venues and platforms simultaneously, market makers must navigate the complexities of arbitrage and order routing. These markets require a holistic understanding of price disparities across different trading venues and the ability to execute trades rapidly to take advantage of these discrepancies. Market makers employ sophisticated algorithms to monitor and respond to price changes across various platforms, ensuring that they can provide seamless liquidity and maintain balanced inventories regardless of where the trade is executed.

Overall, the adaptability of market makers across different market structures underscores their importance in maintaining market efficiency and liquidity. Whether operating in centralized exchanges, dealer markets, ECNs, auction markets, or fragmented markets, market makers employ a combination of strategy, technology, and market insight to perform their vital functions effectively. This versatility not only enhances their role as liquidity providers but also stabilizes the broader financial market system, benefitting all market participants.

5.7   Regulation of Market Makers

In financial markets, market makers play a pivotal role in ensuring liquidity and market efficiency. However, their functions and operations need to be carefully regulated to prevent market abuses and ensure fair trading environments. This section delves into the regulatory frameworks governing market makers, exploring key aspects such as registration requirements, obligations and restrictions, and the overarching regulatory principles that guide their activities.

Market makers are typically subject to stringent registration requirements imposed by national and international regulatory bodies. In the United States, for example, the Securities and Exchange Commission (SEC) mandates that market makers register with a self-regulatory organization (SRO), such as the Financial Industry Regulatory Authority (FINRA). Registration usually entails demonstrating adequate financial stability, technical capability, and adherence to compliance procedures. This process is designed to ensure that only qualified entities are allowed to operate in this capacity, thereby safeguarding the market's integrity.

One of the primary obligations of market makers is to maintain fair and orderly markets. This includes the requirement to provide continuous two-sided quotations—both buy and sell orders—within a specified minimum quote size and spread. The regulatory rationale behind this obligation is to ensure that market makers contribute to market liquidity and price stability. For instance, the SEC's Regulation NMS (National Market System) stipulates that market makers must adhere to certain quoting and trading obligations to promote transparency and fairness.

To mitigate potential conflicts of interest, regulatory authorities impose several restrictions on market makers' operations. Notably, the European Union's Markets in Financial Instruments Directive (MiFID II) includes provisions to separate proprietary trading activities from client-oriented services. This regulation seeks to minimize the risk of market makers exploiting their privileged position to the detriment of market integrity. Additionally, market makers are typically required to report their trading activities to regulatory bodies in real-time, which enhances market surveillance and reduces the risk of manipulative practices.

Regulatory frameworks also emphasize risk management protocols for market makers. Given the inherent risks associated with maintaining large inventories of securities, it is crucial for market makers to employ robust risk management systems. Regulatory guidelines, such as those outlined in the Basel III framework, set forth minimum capital requirements and stress testing procedures to ensure that market makers can withstand market volatility and financial shocks. These requirements are essential to maintain the solvency and operational continuity of market-making firms, thereby contributing to overall market stability.

The overarching regulatory principles guiding market makers' activities are anchored in the concepts of market fairness, transparency, and integrity. Regulatory bodies such as the SEC, the European Securities and Markets Authority (ESMA), and the Financial Conduct Authority (FCA) regularly update and enforce rules to keep pace with the evolving market landscape. This dynamic approach is essential in addressing emerging challenges, such as those posed by high-frequency trading and algorithmic trading strategies. For example, the SEC's Regulation SCI (Systems Compliance and Integrity) mandates that market makers implement comprehensive policies to ensure the resilience of their trading systems against technological failures.

International cooperation among regulators is another critical aspect of the regulatory framework. In an increasingly globalized marketplace, market makers often operate across multiple jurisdictions. Coordinated efforts, such as the Memoranda of Understanding (MOUs) between regulatory bodies, facilitate the sharing of information and the enforcement of consistent regulatory standards globally. This international collaboration helps to prevent regulatory arbitrage, where market makers might exploit less stringent regulations in certain jurisdictions.

In sum, the regulation of market makers is a multifaceted and dynamic domain, designed to balance the need for market liquidity with the imperative of maintaining market integrity and fairness. Through stringent registration processes, operational obligations, risk management requirements, and international cooperation, regulators strive to create a level playing field where market makers can effectively contribute to efficient and orderly markets. By understanding these regulatory frameworks, traders and investors can better appreciate the critical role market makers play in the financial ecosystem.

Chapter 6

High-Frequency Trading

This chapter delves into the realm of high-frequency trading (HFT), exploring its foundational principles and the advanced technology and infrastructure that enable it. It examines various high-frequency trading strategies, highlighting both their advantages and the criticisms they face. The chapter discusses the significant impact HFT has on market dynamics, including liquidity and volatility, and addresses the regulatory challenges it presents. Case studies are included to illustrate real-world applications and outcomes of high-frequency trading in financial markets.

6.1 Basics of High-Frequency Trading

High-Frequency Trading (HFT) is a sophisticated subsection of algorithmic trading that relies on the execution of a large number of orders at extremely high speeds. These trades are typically carried out by powerful computers using complex algorithms to analyze market data and execute trades within fractions of a second. To truly grasp the intricacies of HFT, one must understand its foundational principles, the critical role of speed and time, and the infrastructure that supports it.

HFT firms use algorithms that make decisions about when to buy and sell financial instruments without human intervention. These algorithms are designed to detect minor price discrepancies or market inefficiencies that can be exploited for profit. The sheer volume of transactions and the minimal hold times of positions are defining characteristics of this trading method. Unlike traditional trading, which may consider a wide array of financial fundamentals and hold positions for extended periods, HFT focuses primarily on short-term, technical aspects of price movements.

Central to high-frequency trading is the concept of time. In HFT, milliseconds—or even microseconds—can be the difference between a profitable trade and a loss. This absolute necessity for speed has driven HFT firms to invest heavily in state-of-the-art technology, including high-performance trading platforms, low-latency connectivity, and co-location services. Co-location refers to placing trading servers in the same facility as an exchange's servers to minimize the travel time of data packets, thus reducing latency to nearly imperceptible levels.

The types of strategies employed in high-frequency trading are varied but generally revolve around exploiting the smallest inefficiencies in the market. Some of the most common strategies include market making, statistical arbitrage, and event-driven trading. Market making involves simultaneously placing buy and sell orders for a particular stock to capture the bid-ask spread. Statistical arbitrage entails looking for price patterns or discrepancies that revert to a mean, while event-driven trading capitalizes on news releases or other market-moving information.

Understanding the basics of HFT also requires familiarity with the regulatory landscape, which has evolved dramatically in response to the risks and challenges posed by ultra-fast trading. Regulators worldwide have introduced measures aimed at curbing market manipulation and ensuring fair trading practices. However, due to the rapid pace of technological advancement, the regulatory framework is often playing catch-up with HFT firms that continually seek new ways to gain a competitive edge.

By drawing on a combination of advanced mathematics, state-of-the-art technology, and strategic market insights, high-frequency trading firms are able to execute a large number of trades in the blink of an eye. While the benefits of HFT include enhanced liquidity and tighter spreads, it also presents challenges such as increased market volatility and the potential for systemic risk. As we delve deeper into the technicalities and operational aspects of high-frequency trading in the subsequent sections, it is imperative to keep these foundational principles in mind, recognizing both the enormous potential and the inherent risks associated with this cutting-edge trading approach.

6.2 Technology and Infrastructure

High-Frequency Trading (HFT) is a domain where technological prowess and sophisticated infrastructure are foundational to achieving success. At its core, HFT relies on the capability to process vast amounts of data in microseconds, execute trades at lightning speed, and continuously refine algorithms based on market conditions. This section delves into the critical components of the technology and infrastructure that underpin HFT, providing a detailed understanding suitable for both novice and seasoned investors.

To effectively engage in HFT, firms must invest in and maintain cutting-edge technology. This begins with specialized hardware optimized for speed and efficiency. In the realm of computing hardware, HFT firms utilize Field Programmable Gate Arrays (FPGAs) and Application-Specific Integrated Circuits (ASICs). These are preferred due to their ability to deliver ultra-low latency and high throughput on market data feeds and order executions. FPGAs, in particular, offer customizable hardware configurations that can be fine-tuned to process specific trading algorithms.

The underlying software architecture in HFT is equally critical. High-frequency traders deploy highly optimized trading algorithms written in languages such as C++ and Java, known for their performance and real-time processing capabilities. These algorithms are designed to analyze market data, identify arbitrage opportunities, and execute trades within nanoseconds. Moreover, the software must be adept at handling concurrency, as HFT often involves parallel processing of multiple data streams and execution paths.

Central to the technology stack is the use of low-latency trading platforms. These platforms enable rapid access to market data and facilitate the swift placement of orders. Co-location services provided by exchanges play a vital role here. By placing their servers in close physical proximity to the exchange's servers, HFT firms can reduce the time it takes for their orders to reach the market, cutting down latency to mere microseconds. This proximity to exchanges, combined with direct market access (DMA), provides HFT firms with the advantage of executing trades more quickly than competitors.

Another significant aspect of HFT infrastructure is the connectivity framework. This includes high-speed data feeds and communication networks that can handle the transmission of large volumes of market data with minimal delay. The use of fiber optic cables and, more recently, microwave and millimeter-wave technology, has been instrumental in reducing transmission delays across distances. For international trading, transatlantic and transpacific fiber optic networks provide the backbone for global HFT operations.

Data management and storage solutions are also crucial. Given the sheer volume of data that HFT systems must process and analyze, robust data storage solutions are required. High-frequency traders often rely on Real-Time Data Warehousing systems that allow for the continuous ingestion, processing, and analysis of streaming data. Additionally, the use of Non-Volatile Memory Express (NVMe) storage devices ensures that data retrieval times are minimized, supporting the rapid decision-making processes inherent to HFT.

In the context of HFT, security and resilience are paramount. Ensuring the protection of trading systems from cyber threats requires sophisticated security measures, including advanced encryption protocols, multi-factor authentication, and regular penetration testing. Moreover, the infrastructure must be designed with redundancy to handle system failures gracefully. This entails the use of redundant hardware, backup power supplies, and disaster recovery plans to ensure continued operations under adverse conditions.

Another cornerstone of an HFT setup is the algorithmic strategy employed. These strategies must be continuously refined and adapted to changing market conditions. Machine learning and artificial intelligence play a significant role in modern HFT, allowing for the development of adaptive algorithms that enhance prediction accuracy and trade execution efficiency. By utilizing historical and real-time data, these algorithms can learn and evolve, improving their performance over time.

Furthermore, the symbiotic relationship between hardware, software, and networking components drives the relentless pursuit of speed and efficiency in HFT. This necessitates a continuous cycle of innovation and upgrade, where obsolete technologies are swiftly replaced by newer, faster, and more efficient alternatives.

In sum, the technology and infrastructure supporting HFT are complex and multifaceted. They encompass specialized hardware, cutting-edge software, low-latency platforms, high-speed connectivity, robust data management, stringent security protocols, and resilient systems design. Together, these elements form the backbone of high-frequency trading, enabling firms to process vast amounts of information, execute trades in microseconds, and continuously adapt to the evolving market landscape. As technology advances, the infrastructure supporting HFT will undoubtedly continue to evolve, setting new benchmarks for speed and efficiency in financial markets.

6.3   Strategies Used in High-Frequency Trading

In the intricate world of high-frequency trading (HFT), a variety of strategies are employed to capitalize on market opportunities that occur at microsecond speeds. These strategies harness the power of cutting-edge technology and sophisticated algorithms to execute trades with unprecedented speed and precision. Understanding these strategies provides insight into the mechanics that drive HFT, and the subtle yet powerful ways in which they influence financial markets.

One prevalent strategy in HFT is market making. Market makers continuously provide liquidity to the market by submitting buy and sell limit orders for a specific set of securities. They profit from the bid-ask spread—the difference between the price at which they are willing to buy (the bid) and the price at which they are willing to sell (the ask). High-frequency market makers lever their advanced systems to rapidly update quotes in response to market movements and trade orders. This requires robust technology capable of monitoring the market in real time to adjust prices and manage inventory efficiently.

Arbitrage is another cornerstone strategy in HFT, exploiting price discrepancies of the same asset across different markets or in different forms. For instance, in statistical arbitrage, sophisticated mathematical models identify temporary deviations from historical price relationships between correlated securities. High-frequency traders then execute trades to profit from the anticipated convergence of these prices. Similarly, in cross-exchange arbitrage, traders leverage latency differences between exchanges to buy at a lower price in one market and sell at a higher price in another, all within fractions of a second. This strategy demands low-latency connections and accurate synchronization between trading venues.

Momentum ignition strategies seek to initiate or intensify short-term price trends, enabling traders to capitalize on resulting price movements. This involves submitting a series of small orders designed to trigger the execution of large block trades by other participants, thereby driving the price in a favorable direction. Once the momentum is believed to have been ignited, high-frequency traders then take advantage of this volatility by quickly reversing their position to gain from the induced price swings.

Liquidity detection strategies, also known as sniffing, aim to identify hidden liquidity within the market. These strategies use specialized algorithms to detect large orders that are being executed incrementally (also known as iceberg orders) to avoid detection. By sensing these orders, high-frequency traders can trade ahead of, or in conjunction with, these large orders to capture profits from anticipated price movements once the orders become visible to the broader market.

Another sophisticated approach is latency arbitrage, where speed is the significant edge. In this strategy, traders exploit the time delay (latency) in the dissemination of market data between different participants. This involves high investments in state-of-the-art technology to achieve minimal latency, effectively allowing traders to see market movements on one exchange before other market participants and act accordingly on another exchange.

To enhance transparency and understandability, it is important to present a simplified example of statistical arbitrage. Consider two highly correlated stocks, Stock A and Stock B. Over the past three months, the price ratio of these two stocks has remained relatively stable. However, an unusual event causes Stock A to rapidly decrease in price while Stock B remains stable. High-frequency traders identify this deviation from the historical ratio and immediately buy Stock A while shorting Stock B. As market adjustments occur and the prices of the two stocks converge back to their historical relationship, the traders close their positions, capturing a profit from this reversion.

Implementing these advanced strategies requires robust infrastructure, including co-location services to place HFT servers as close as possible to exchange servers, minimizing latency. Furthermore, traders depend heavily on high-speed data feeds and low-latency execution strategies to maintain competitiveness. Continuous advancements in hardware, such as field-programmable gate arrays (FPGAs), and software, including predictive analytics and machine learning, are key components in maintaining and enhancing the effectiveness of HFT strategies.

Each strategy discussed exhibits unique advantages and vulnerabilities. For instance, market making fosters liquidity but exposes the trader to inventory risk during volatile markets. Arbitrage ensures market efficiency but may fail in instances of significant market regime changes. Momentum ignition and liquidity detection can be highly profitable yet are scrutinized heavily by regulatory entities due to their potential impact on market fairness.

By delving into these strategies, we gain a comprehensive understanding of the tools and techniques that high-frequency traders employ to outpace traditional market participants. Such insights underscore the significant role that technology and algorithmic precision play in the evolving landscape of financial markets, illustrating the dynamic interplay between speed, strategy, and market structure.

6.4   Benefits and Criticisms of HFT

High-Frequency Trading (HFT) stands at the intersection of technology and finance, playing a critical role in the dynamics of modern financial markets. While it has brought numerous advantages to the trading ecosystem, it also faces considerable scrutiny and criticism. This section explores the multifaceted benefits and challenges associated with HFT, providing a balanced perspective to help readers understand the complexities and implications of this trading model.

Benefits of HFT:

One of the primary advantages of HFT is its contribution to increased market liquidity. High-frequency traders execute a large number of transactions in a very short time, often buying and selling securities to capture small price discrepancies. This continuous flow of orders helps to narrow the bid-ask spread, making it cheaper for other market participants to trade. The presence of HFT firms can thus enhance market depth and reduce transaction costs for all traders.

Another significant benefit is the improvement in market efficiency. HFT algorithms are designed to exploit inefficiencies and arbitrage opportunities across different markets. By swiftly correcting price discrepancies, these algorithms facilitate a more accurate representation of asset values. This constant adjustment ensures that prices reflect all available information promptly, contributing to the overall integrity and functionality of financial markets.

Speed and precision are also hallmarks of HFT. The ability to process large volumes of data and execute trades within milliseconds minimizes the latency that can lead to market distortions. High-frequency traders use sophisticated algorithms to analyze market conditions and react instantaneously, providing a form of liquidity that is both reliable and responsive. This high-speed trading helps stabilize markets by dampening volatility and absorbing shocks more effectively.

Furthermore, HFT has driven technological advancements in the financial industry. The competitive nature of high-frequency trading has spurred investments in state-of-the-art hardware and software, contributing to the overall progress of financial technology. Enhanced data analytics, improved network infrastructure, and cutting-edge trading platforms are some of the byproducts of the HFT boom, benefiting the broader market by elevating the standard of technological innovation.

Criticisms of HFT:

Despite its advantages, HFT has not been without controversy. One of the most prominent criticisms is its potential to contribute to market volatility. While HFT can absorb and mitigate price fluctuations to some extent, the sheer volume and speed of trades can, paradoxically, amplify short-term volatility. Instances like the 2010 Flash Crash illustrate how HFT algorithms can react to unexpected market conditions in ways that exacerbate rapid price movements, leading to significant market disruptions.

The fairness of HFT practices is also a major concern. High-frequency traders often have access to superior technology and information, including low-latency connections that give them a timing advantage over other market participants. This informational asymmetry raises questions about market equity and whether retail investors are disadvantaged by the presence of HFT firms. Critics argue that HFT firms may capitalize on their speed to execute front-running strategies, undermining the fairness of the trading environment.

Regulatory challenges are another critical issue tied to HFT. The rapid execution of trades poses significant monitoring difficulties for regulatory bodies, which may struggle to keep pace with the evolving landscape of high-frequency trading. Ensuring that HFT practices adhere to legal and ethical standards without stifling innovation is a delicate balancing act for regulators worldwide. The complexity and opacity of HFT algorithms further complicate the task of identifying and mitigating potentially harmful activities.

Additionally, HFT can lead to increased market fragmentation. The pursuit of speed has driven the proliferation of multiple trading venues, including dark pools and alternative trading systems (ATS). While this fragmentation can provide greater liquidity and trading opportunities, it also complicates market structure and may obscure price discovery processes. The dispersion of orders across various platforms can lead to a lack of transparency, where the true state of the market is harder to discern for both regulators and participants.

Finally, the substantial resources required for HFT can contribute to a concentration of trading power among a few well-capitalized firms. The costs associated with developing and maintaining HFT infrastructure, including data centers, high-speed networks, and sophisticated algorithms, create high barriers to entry. This concentration can reduce market competition and increase the influence of a limited number of players over market dynamics.

High-Frequency Trading undeniably offers several benefits to the financial markets, including enhanced liquidity, improved efficiency, and technological innovation. However, its criticisms, such as contributing to volatility, unfair practices, regulatory challenges, market fragmentation, and concentration of power, highlight the complexity of its role. These challenges underscore the necessity for ongoing dialogue between industry stakeholders and regulators to ensure that the advantages of HFT are realized while mitigating its potential downsides. The following section on the impact of HFT on market dynamics will delve deeper into how these benefits and criticisms manifest in real-world trading environments.

6.5   Impact of HFT on Market Dynamics

High-Frequency Trading (HFT) has been a transformative force in the financial markets. Its effects on market dynamics are profound and multifaceted, influencing various aspects such as liquidity, volatility, price discovery, and the overall trading environment. This section will explore these impacts in detail, consolidating knowledge for both novice traders and seasoned professionals.

At its core, HFT operates at the intersection of speed and volume. The rapid execution of trades within fractions of a second allows high-frequency traders to capitalize on minute price discrepancies, contributing significantly to market liquidity. Liquidity, defined as the ease with which assets can be bought or sold in the market without affecting the asset's price, is a critical component of healthy financial markets. HFT firms typically submit a substantial number of orders, many of which are limit orders that rest on the order book to be filled at predetermined prices. This behavior enhances liquidity by increasing the number of buy and sell orders available at various price levels, thereby narrowing bid-ask spreads.

$$\text{Bid-Ask Spread} = \text{Ask Price} - \text{Bid Price}$$

By narrowing the bid-ask spread, HFT activities reduce transaction costs for all market participants. A lower bid-ask spread implies that traders get better prices whether buying or selling, which can be particularly beneficial for retail investors who may not have the same technological advantages as HFT firms. However, this augmentation of liquidity is not without its caveats. The liquidity provided by HFT can be ephemeral, vanishing quickly in times of market stress or heightened volatility.

Volatility, a statistical measure of the dispersion of returns for a given security or market index, is another crucial aspect influenced by HFT. While there is ongoing debate regarding the extent of HFT's impact on market volatility, it is generally acknowledged that HFT can both dampen and exacerbate volatility under different circumstances. On one hand, the swift and continuous trading by HFT firms can absorb shocks and provide immediate counterbalancing trades, thus stabilizing prices. On the other hand, during periods of high stress or in response to erroneous trading algorithms, HFT activities can amplify price movements, contributing to "flash crashes" or rapid, large-scale price corrections.

$$\text{Volatility} = \sqrt{\sum_{i=1}^{N} \frac{(R_i - \overline{R})^2}{N-1}}$$

Here, R_i represents individual return observations and $\overline{R}$ is the mean return over N observations.

The role of HFT in price discovery, the process by which the market determines the price of an asset through the interaction of supply and demand, is another area where its impact is noteworthy. High-frequency traders often engage in market-making and arbitrage strategies that adjust to new information almost instantaneously. This rapid incorporation of information into asset prices contributes to market efficiency, ensuring that prices more accurately reflect underlying fundamentals.

However, this accelerated pace also introduces complexities. The information advantage held by HFT firms can potentially undermine the position of traditional market participants, particularly those who rely on slower, more traditional methods of receiving and processing market data. Consequently, the competitive landscape shifts, favoring those equipped with advanced technology and sophisticated algorithms.

Moreover, the presence of HFT has induced structural changes in market infrastructure. Exchanges and trading venues have evolved to accommodate the demands of high-frequency traders, from implementing low-latency systems to providing colocation services. While these advancements facilitate faster and more efficient trading, they also raise critical questions about market fairness and accessibility. Smaller participants may find themselves at a disadvantage, unable to compete with the speed and precision of HFT entities.

Lastly, the influence of HFT extends to the broader trading environment. The sheer volume of orders generated by HFT can contribute to market noise, making it challenging for traditional traders to differentiate between genuine price signals and transient fluctuations. This phenomenon necessitates refined analytical tools and strategies for non-HFT participants to navigate the increasingly complex landscape effectively.

In examining the overall impact of HFT on market dynamics, it is essential to recognize the dual nature of its effects. While HFT brings significant benefits, such as enhanced liquidity, tighter spreads, and more efficient price discovery, it also presents challenges that regulators, exchanges, and market participants must address. Balancing these elements is crucial for maintaining robust and equitable financial markets.

Understanding these dynamics empowers traders and investors to make informed decisions, leveraging the advantages of HFT while mitigating its potential downsides. Through continuous study and adaptation, market participants can navigate the intricate interplay of factors influenced by high-frequency trading, fostering a healthy and dynamic trading environment.

6.6 Regulatory Environment

High-frequency trading (HFT), situated at the nexus of finance and technology, operates within a complex regulatory landscape that aims to ensure fair, transparent, and efficient markets. Regulatory bodies worldwide have recognized the unique challenges and risks posed by HFT and have imposed various rules and guidelines to mitigate these concerns. Understanding the regulatory environment is crucial for both market participants and policymakers in fostering a stable trading ecosystem.

The advent and rapid evolution of HFT prompted regulators to reassess existing frameworks and implement new measures tailored to the high-speed nature of algorithmic trading. Key regulatory bodies, including the Securities and Exchange Commission (SEC) in the United States, the European Securities and Markets Authority (ESMA), and the Financial Conduct Authority (FCA) in the United Kingdom, have led efforts to address the peculiarities of HFT.

One of the foundational regulatory responses to HFT in the United States was the implementation of the Regulation National Market System (Reg NMS) in 2007 by the SEC. Reg NMS was designed to modernize and strengthen the national market system for equity securities. It introduced rules such as the Order Protection Rule, which aims to prevent trade-throughs—trades at prices worse than the best available quotes. While not exclusively targeted at HFT, Reg NMS facilitated its growth by standardizing trading practices across multiple venues and reducing latency arbitrage opportunities.

In Europe, the Markets in Financial Instruments Directive II (MiFID II), which came into effect in January 2018, represents another significant regulatory effort. MiFID II encompasses a broad range of provisions aimed at enhancing market transparency and curbing excesses attributed to HFT. Key aspects include algorithmic trading requirements, such as the obligation for firms engaged in HFT to be authorized by regulatory bodies, maintain robust risk controls, and ensure the resilience of their trading systems. Furthermore, MiFID II mandates pre-and post-trade transparency to improve market integrity.

Another critical aspect of the regulatory environment is the focus on market abuse and manipulation prevention. HFT firms are subject to stringent surveillance to detect and prevent manipulative practices like spoofing (placing orders with the intent to cancel before execution) and layering (submitting multiple orders at different price levels to create a false impression of demand or supply). For instance, the Dodd-Frank Wall Street Reform and Consumer Protection Act in the United States has provisions that specifically address such abusive behaviors in financial markets.

Globally, regulatory cooperation has also been instrumental in managing the cross-border implications of HFT. The International Organization of Securities Commissions (IOSCO) plays a pivotal role in coordinating efforts among different jurisdictions to harmonize regulatory standards and share best practices. This collaboration is crucial in an era where trading activity transcends national boundaries, ensuring that regulatory actions in one market do not inadvertently create vulnerabilities in another.

Regulation in the HFT space is not static but continually evolving as market structures, technology, and trading strategies advance. One notable trend is the increasing use of technology by regulators themselves to monitor and analyze market activity. Market surveillance systems employing sophisticated algorithms and real-time data analytics are becoming standard tools for regulators to detect anomalies and enforce compliance more effectively.

To illustrate the fluid nature of the regulatory environment, the SEC's Rule 15c3-5, known as the Market Access Rule, was introduced to address the risks associated with direct market access (DMA) and sponsored access arrangements. This rule requires brokers and dealers to implement risk management controls and supervisory procedures to prevent erroneous trades and ensure compliance with regulatory requirements. Such measures are reflective of the iterative process where regulators refine rules to keep pace with market developments.

From a compliance perspective, HFT firms must navigate these regulations meticulously to avoid penalties and maintain their trading privileges. This often involves significant investments in legal advisory, compliance infrastructure, and continuous monitoring systems. Firms may also engage in dialogue with regulators, contributing to the development of rules and gaining insights into regulatory expectations.

While the regulatory environment surrounding HFT is multifaceted and occasionally contentious, it aims to balance innovation with the safeguarding of market integrity. Regulatory measures strive to mitigate system-wide risks and protect investors while accommodating the efficiency gains brought by high-frequency trading. By fostering a transparent and equitable trading landscape, regulators play an indispensable role in the sustainable evolution of financial markets. Through adherence to these regulatory frameworks, HFT can continue to contribute to market liquidity and price discovery in a manner that upholds the principles of fair and orderly markets.

6.7   Case Studies in High-Frequency Trading

In this section, we will investigate real-world applications and outcomes of high-frequency trading (HFT) through a series of insightful case studies. These case studies illuminate the intricate mechanisms of HFT, the strategies employed, and the resultant impact on financial markets. By examining these scenarios, we gain a deeper understanding of both the potential benefits and pitfalls associated with high-frequency trading.

Case Study 1: The Flash Crash of May 6, 2010

Perhaps one of the most infamous incidents associated with HFT is the Flash Crash of May 6, 2010. On this day, U.S. equity markets experienced an unprecedented plunge and subsequent rebound within a span of mere minutes. The Dow Jones Industrial Average dropped about 1,000 points, which was nearly 9% of its value, before quickly recovering.

Detailed analysis revealed that a key factor in this dramatic event was a feedback loop triggered by a large sell order executed by a mutual fund. This order was managed by an algorithm designed to trade aggressively without consideration for prevailing market conditions. High-frequency traders responded to this sell pressure by rapidly amplifying its effects through their strategies, exacerbating the liquidity vacuum.

The key factors identified in this case include:

- **Aggressive Algorithmic Trading:** The aggressive sales tactics of the mutual fund's algorithm were not suited to the market conditions, leading to immediate liquidity absorption.

- **Liquidity Vacuum:** The abrupt withdrawal of high-frequency traders from the market increased volatility and diminished available liquidity.

- **Feedback Loops:** The rapid, automated responses from HFT systems intensified price movements, creating a cycle that magnified the initial shock.

This incident highlighted the need for robust risk management systems, greater scrutiny of trading algorithms, and improved coordination among market participants to prevent similar occurrences.

Case Study 2: Virtu Financial's Consistent Profitability

Virtu Financial is a notable firm in the high-frequency trading arena, known for its remarkable consistency in profitability. Over a five-year period, Virtu reportedly had only one losing trading day, a testament to its sophisticated HFT algorithms and trading strategies.

Virtu's success can be attributed to several key practices:

- **Diversification Across Markets:** Virtu diversifies its trades across numerous markets and asset classes, reducing exposure to sector-specific risks.

- **Advanced Technology:** The firm leverages state-of-the-art technology to ensure minimal latency in trade execution, gaining competitive advantages through speed.

- **Market Making:** By providing liquidity and earning the bid-ask spread, Virtu creates a stable revenue stream while contributing to market efficiency.

The consistency shown by Virtu Financial underlines the potential for successful implementation of high-frequency trading strategies when paired with appropriate market knowledge, technological infrastructure, and comprehensive risk management.

Case Study 3: Knight Capital's Trading Glitch

On August 1, 2012, Knight Capital Group encountered a software issue that led to errant trades amounting to over $440 million in losses within 45 minutes. This event underscores the critical importance of technological robustness and the risk of systemic errors in HFT.

Key lessons from Knight Capital's glitch include:

- **Software Reliability and Testing:** Inadequate testing and updates to trading algorithms can result in catastrophic errors, highlighting the need for rigorous quality assurance and continuous monitoring.

- **Risk Management:** Robust fail-safes and instant trade halting mechanisms are essential to mitigate potential losses from unforeseen technical glitches.

- **System Resilience:** Building resilient systems that can swiftly detect and recover from errors can prevent minor issues from snowballing into significant financial disasters.

The Knight Capital episode serves as a stark reminder of the vulnerabilities inherent in automated trading systems and the necessity of stringent operational controls.

The aforementioned case studies offer valuable insights into the dynamics and consequences of high-frequency trading. They exemplify both the prowess and the perils associated with the rapid evolution of financial markets driven by technological advancements. By learning from these real-world events, traders and regulatory bodies can better understand how to harness the benefits of HFT while mitigating its risks.

Chapter 7

Market Structure and Regulation

This chapter provides an overview of various market structures, contrasting exchange-based markets with over-the-counter (OTC) markets. It identifies key regulatory bodies and outlines the evolution of regulatory frameworks that govern market activities. The chapter discusses compliance and reporting requirements, along with the broader impact of regulation on market behavior and dynamics. Additionally, it explores global differences in market regulation, emphasizing how these disparities influence cross-border trading and market practices.

7.1   Overview of Market Structures

Understanding the varied landscape of market structures is crucial for both novice and seasoned investors. Market structures provide the framework within which trading activities occur, and they significantly influence the efficiency, liquidity, and transparency of transactions. Broadly, financial markets can be categorized into two primary types: exchange-based markets and over-the-counter (OTC) markets. Each of these markets has distinct characteristics, operational mechanisms, and regulatory environments.

Exchange-based markets are centralized venues where securities, commodities, derivatives, and other financial instruments are traded. These markets are characterized by their high levels of regulation, standardized contracts, and transparent pricing mechanisms. The New York Stock Exchange (NYSE) and the NASDAQ are prominent examples of exchange-based markets. One of the key features of these markets is the centralized order book, which aggregates buy and sell orders, providing a clear view of market depth and facilitating efficient price discovery. Traders in exchange-based markets benefit from the high liquidity and minimized counterparty risk due to the presence of clearinghouses that guarantee the settlement of trades.

In contrast, OTC markets operate in a decentralized manner, where trades are conducted directly between two parties without the intermediation of an exchange. This market structure offers greater flexibility in terms of contract customization and trading hours, catering to the needs of entities that require tailored financial instruments or operate in less liquid markets. However, the decentralized nature of OTC markets also introduces higher counterparty risk, as there is no central clearinghouse to ensure trade settlement. Examples of instruments typically traded in the OTC market include corporate bonds, foreign exchange, and certain derivatives.

Market structure also influences the liquidity and transparency of trading activities. In exchange-based markets, liquidity is generally higher due to the aggregation of a large number of participants and standardized products. Transparency is also a significant advantage, as the centralized order book provides visibility into market depth and recent trade prices, fostering confidence among investors. Conversely, the OTC market's decentralized nature results in lower transparency, as trades are often negotiated privately and details are not immediately disseminated to the broader market. Liquidity in OTC markets can also be more variable, depending significantly on the specific instrument and the number of active participants.

The role of technology in modern market structures cannot be overstated. Automated trading systems and algorithmic trading have revolutionized the speed and efficiency with which trades are executed. High-frequency trading (HFT), a subset of algorithmic trading, takes advantage of minute price discrepancies across different markets or instruments, often executing thousands of trades within milliseconds. While this has brought about increased liquidity and tighter spreads, it has also raised regulatory and ethical questions concerning market fairness and stability.

Regulation plays a pivotal role in shaping market structures. Exchange-based markets are subject to stringent regulatory requirements, including regular reporting, compliance checks, and oversight by governmental or self-regulatory organizations. In the United States, the Securities and Exchange Commission (SEC) and Financial Industry Regulatory Authority (FINRA) oversee the activities of exchange-based markets, ensuring that they operate fairly and transparently. OTC markets, while less regulated in terms of day-to-day operations, are still subject to regulatory oversight to ensure the integrity of the financial system, particularly with regard to preventing systemic risk and promoting market stability.

Understanding the nuances of different market structures equips investors with the knowledge to navigate the complexities of financial markets more effectively. By recognizing the inherent advantages and risks associated with each type of market, traders can make informed decisions that align with their investment objectives and risk tolerance. Whether an investor prefers the transparency and liquidity of exchange-based markets or the flexibility of OTC markets, a comprehensive understanding of these structures is essential for successful trading and investing.

The subsequent sections will delve deeper into the specificities of exchange and OTC markets, providing a detailed comparison that highlights the practical implications for market participants. The exploration of key regulatory bodies and the evolution of regulatory frameworks will further illuminate how these structures are maintained and monitored, ensuring the robustness and integrity of the global financial system.

7.2 Differences between Exchange and OTC Markets

Understanding the distinctions between exchange-based markets and over-the-counter (OTC) markets is crucial for any investor aiming to navigate the financial landscape effectively. These two primary market structures offer different trading environments, regulatory frameworks, and implications for liquidity, transparency, and risk. This section delves deeply into these differences, providing clarity on their respective advantages and potential pitfalls.

Exchange-based markets, also known as centralized markets, are formal organizations that facilitate the trading of securities in a transparent and regulated environment. Examples include the New York Stock Exchange (NYSE), NASDAQ, and the London Stock Exchange (LSE). These exchanges provide a centralized location, usually digital nowadays, where buyers and sellers can execute trades under rules established by the exchange itself and regulatory authorities.

One of the primary benefits of trading on an exchange is the high level of transparency. Exchange-based markets are required to disclose trade prices, volumes, and other relevant data almost instantaneously. This transparency helps to ensure a fair trading environment and can significantly reduce information asymmetry between different market participants. For instance, the bid-ask spread, which represents the difference between the highest price a buyer is willing to pay and the lowest price a seller is willing to accept, is generally narrower in exchange-based markets due to higher liquidity and more participants.

Exchanges also provide mechanisms to mitigate counterparty risk. This is typically achieved through the use of clearinghouses, which act as intermediaries between buyers and sellers, ensuring that both parties fulfill their contractual obligations. By guaranteeing the completion of trades, clearinghouses enhance market stability and investor confidence.

In contrast, over-the-counter (OTC) markets operate in a decentralized manner without the centralized infrastructure of an exchange. Trades in the OTC market occur directly between two parties, often through a network of dealers who negotiate prices and terms. This market structure is common for, but not limited to, less liquid securities, derivative contracts, and certain fixed-income securities, such as corporate bonds and municipal bonds.

One of the key characteristics of OTC markets is their flexibility. Because trading happens directly between parties, OTC markets can accommodate bespoke and complex transactions that might not fit within the standardized formats required by exchanges. This flexibility makes OTC markets particularly attractive for institutional investors looking for customized financial products and for companies seeking to hedge specific risks.

However, this decentralized nature also introduces certain drawbacks. OTC markets often suffer from lower transparency compared to exchange-based markets. Trade details are typically not disclosed publicly, leading to greater opacity. This absence of transparency can result in wider bid-ask spreads, as dealers incorporate a premium to compensate for the higher risk and lower liquidity. Additionally, the lack of a central clearinghouse in many OTC transactions means that counterparty risk is more pronounced. Parties must rely on each other's creditworthiness, increasing the potential for default.

Regulatory oversight also differs significantly between exchange and OTC markets. Exchanges are subject to stringent regulatory requirements imposed by both governmental agencies and the exchanges themselves. These regulations aim to protect investors, ensure market integrity, and maintain orderly market conditions. In contrast, OTC markets, while still regulated, generally face less stringent oversight. The regulatory focus in OTC markets tends to be on the financial soundness and reporting standards of dealers rather than the transactions themselves.

For example, the Dodd-Frank Wall Street Reform and Consumer Protection Act in the United States introduced several reforms aimed at increasing transparency and reducing systemic risk in the OTC derivatives market. One of the key provisions is the requirement for certain standardized OTC derivatives to be cleared through central counterparties and reported to trade repositories.

The differences between exchange and OTC markets also manifest in terms of market participants. Exchange-based markets typically attract a wide variety of participants, including retail investors, institutional investors, market makers, and high-frequency trading firms. This broad mix of participants contributes to high liquidity and enhances the price discovery process. In contrast, the OTC market primarily involves institutional investors and large financial entities, such as banks and hedge funds, conducting large volume trades.

In conclusion, both exchange-based and OTC markets offer unique benefits and challenges. Exchange-based markets provide high levels of transparency, liquidity, and reduced counterparty risk, which can be advantageous for typical equity trades and more standardized financial instruments. OTC markets, with their flexibility and capacity for customized transactions, are essential for certain types of trades and financial products but come with increased opacity and counterparty risk. Understanding these differences allows investors to choose the market structure that best suits their trading strategy, risk tolerance, and investment goals.

7.3 Key Regulatory Bodies

Understanding the key regulatory bodies that oversee market activities is fundamental to comprehending the intricate dynamics of financial markets. These organizations create, implement, and enforce regulations that ensure the market operates smoothly, fairly, and transparently, thereby protecting investor interests and maintaining systemic stability.

First, we examine the role of regulatory bodies at a domestic level. In the United States, the primary regulatory authorities include the Securities and Exchange Commission (SEC) and the Commodity Futures Trading Commission (CFTC).

The SEC is tasked with regulating the securities markets, including stocks and bonds. Its mission is to protect investors, maintain fair, orderly, and efficient markets, and facilitate capital formation. To achieve these goals, the SEC enforces a body of law known as securities law, which governs the disclosure of information by public companies, the conduct of securities professionals, and the trading activities of securities markets. For instance, the SEC mandates that publicly traded companies regularly disclose financial and other significant information that might impact an investor's decision-making process. This transparency helps reduce the risk of fraud and manipulative practices, fostering investor confidence.

The CFTC, on the other hand, oversees the derivatives markets, including futures, options, and swaps. The CFTC's role is to promote competitive and efficient markets while protecting market participants against fraud, manipulation, and abusive practices. The commission establishes regulations covering everything from market transparency to the behavior of traders and exchanges. For example, the CFTC enforces position limits designed to prevent excessive speculation, which can lead to market distortions.

Beyond the national framework, global financial markets are monitored by international regulatory bodies. The International Organization of Securities Commissions (IOSCO) and the Basel Committee on Banking Supervision (BCBS) are two prominent examples.

IOSCO sets the global standards for securities regulation. It brings together the world's securities regulators and establishes principles and guidelines aimed at improving market transparency, enhancing investor protection, and reducing systemic risk. By harmonizing rules across jurisdictions, IOSCO facilitates international collaboration and helps mitigate the risks associated with cross-border trading. For instance, IOSCO's Multilateral Memorandum of Understanding (MMoU) provides a structured mechanism for cooperation and information exchange among regulators, which is crucial in addressing issues like market manipulation and insider trading on an international scale.

The BCBS, under the Bank for International Settlements (BIS), focuses primarily on enhancing the quality of banking supervision worldwide. While it does not have direct regulatory authority, its guidelines and frameworks, such as the Basel III accords, have a significant impact on national banking regulations. These guidelines aim to strengthen bank capital requirements, improve risk management practices, and enhance the resilience of the banking sector. Through initiatives like these, the BCBS ensures that banks operate securely and can withstand financial stresses, thus contributing to global financial stability.

On a regional scale, the European Securities and Markets Authority (ESMA) plays a crucial role within the European Union. ESMA not only ensures financial market stability within the EU but also improves investor protection and enhances cooperation among national regulatory authorities. It develops a unified rule book for EU financial markets, minimizing regulatory arbitrage and fostering consistency across member states. For example, ESMA's guidelines on market abuse regulation provide a framework to detect, enforce, and sanction market abuse, copying methodologies that enhance the integrity of the EU financial markets.

Similarly, other regions have equivalent bodies; for instance, the Financial Conduct Authority (FCA) in the UK and the Australia Securities and Investments Commission (ASIC). Each of these authorities tailors its approach to the unique financial and economic landscape of its jurisdiction while aligning, where possible, with international standards to ensure seamless market operations and minimize disruption.

Given the complexity and interconnectedness of today's financial markets, the role of regulatory bodies is paramount in ensuring orderly market functioning. Their efforts to harmonize regulations and standardize practices across borders also play a significant part in mitigating systemic risks and fostering a stable global financial environment. By adhering to the frameworks and guidelines set forth by these regulatory authorities, market participants can navigate the financial landscape more effectively and with greater confidence.

7.4 Regulatory Frameworks and Their Evolution

The regulatory landscape of financial markets has undergone significant transformation over the decades, guided by the need to balance market efficiency, investor protection, and systemic stability. Understanding the evolution of regulatory frameworks provides insight into why modern markets operate the way they do and offers a blueprint for anticipating future regulatory shifts.

Early financial markets operated with minimal oversight, and regulation primarily emerged in response to crises. The stock market crash of 1929, which precipitated the Great Depression, marked a pivotal moment in the United States. In response, several landmark legislations were enacted, establishing the foundational regulatory framework we recognize today.

The Securities Act of 1933 was designed to restore investor confidence by ensuring greater transparency in financial statements, thereby reducing the risk of fraud. This Act mandated that issuers provide detailed and accurate financial information via registration statements and prospectuses. The following year saw the introduction of the Securities Exchange Act of 1934, which established the Securities and Exchange Commission (SEC). The SEC's role was to enforce securities laws and regulate stock exchanges, securities, and other financial markets. This formalized the oversight of market activities, ensuring market integrity and investor protection.

In the decades that followed, financial markets evolved, growing more complex with the advent of new financial products and technologies. The regulatory frameworks had to adapt correspondingly. For instance, the Investment Advisers Act of 1940 sought to regulate the actions of investment advisers, ensuring they acted in the best interests of their clients, while the Investment Company Act of 1940 aimed to regulate mutual funds and other investment companies.

In the 1970s and 1980s, deregulation trends emerged, fueled by the belief in market efficiency and the benefits of free markets. This period saw significant deregulation in financial markets, most notably the repeal of fixed commission rates in 1975 through the Securities Acts Amendments. This led to greater competition among brokerage firms and the development of discount brokers. Additionally, the Garn-St. Germain Depository Institutions Act of 1982 deregulated savings and loan associations, which had significant long-term implications.

The 1990s and early 2000s were marked by the globalization of financial markets and the rise of complex derivative products. Legislation such as the Gramm-Leach-Bliley Act of 1999 repealed parts of the Glass-Steagall Act, breaking down barriers between commercial banking, investment banking, and insurance services. This facilitated the creation of diversified financial institutions but also increased systemic risk, as evidenced by the financial crisis that unfolded nearly a decade later.

The collapse of Lehman Brothers in 2008 and the subsequent global financial crisis underscored the weaknesses in the then-existing regulatory framework. The crisis prompted a significant overhaul of financial regulation worldwide. In the United States, the Dodd-Frank Wall Street Reform and Consumer Protection Act of 2010 implemented comprehensive reforms aimed at reducing risks in the financial system. Key provisions included the establishment of the Consumer Financial Protection Bureau (CFPB), the introduction of the Volcker Rule to restrict proprietary trading by banks, and enhanced oversight of financial institutions deemed "too big to fail."

Internationally, the Basel III accords were developed to strengthen regulation, supervision, and risk management within the banking sector. Basel III introduced more stringent capital requirements, leverage ratios, and liquidity requirements to fortify banks against economic shocks.

More recently, regulatory frameworks have had to adapt to technological advancements, such as high-frequency trading (HFT) and cryptocurrency markets. Regulations like the European Union's Markets in Financial Instruments Directive II (MiFID II), implemented in 2018, aimed to increase transparency in financial markets and improve protections for investors, especially in response to HFT practices and dark pools.

The evolution of regulatory frameworks undeniably reflects a continuous balancing act: adapting to market innovations while safeguarding against systemic risks and protecting investors. Future regulatory developments will likely focus on areas such as artificial intelligence in trading, data privacy concerns, and the growing influence of fintech and decentralized finance (DeFi) platforms. By appreciating the historical context and underlying motivations behind regulatory changes, market participants can better navigate and anticipate the regulatory landscape.

Understanding this evolution highlights the dynamic interplay between market innovations and regulatory oversight, shaping the future of trading and investing.

7.5 Compliance and Reporting Requirements

Compliance and reporting requirements form the backbone of a well-functioning financial market, ensuring transparency, fairness, and integrity. Institutions operating within these markets must adhere to a complex web of regulations designed to prevent fraudulent activities, market manipulation, and systemic risks. Clear understanding and diligent implementation of these requirements are crucial for market participants, from individual investors to large financial firms. Let us delve into the key aspects of compliance and reporting within financial markets, unpacking the obligations they impose and the mechanisms through which they are enforced.

The primary objective of compliance is to ensure that market participants adhere to the rules and regulations set forth by regulatory bodies. This includes maintaining standards of conduct, operational integrity, and protecting investor interests. The framework of compliance is multi-faceted, incorporating both preventive measures and corrective actions to address potential violations. Institutions typically establish dedicated compliance departments tasked with monitoring, administering, and enforcing compliance policies.

One fundamental aspect of compliance is the Know Your Customer (KYC) requirement. This mandates that financial institutions verify the identity of their clients to deter money laundering, terrorist financing, and other illicit activities. KYC processes involve collecting and verifying information such as identification documents, residential addresses, and financial backgrounds. Institutions must maintain accurate records and regularly update these details to ensure ongoing compliance.

Another critical component is the Anti-Money Laundering (AML) regulations, which extend beyond KYC to encompass broader measures aimed at detecting and preventing money laundering activities. Financial institutions are required to implement AML programs that include transaction monitoring, reporting of suspicious activities, and maintaining controls to mitigate risks associated with money laundering. The AML framework often necessitates advanced technologies and sophisticated algorithms to identify and flag unusual patterns indicative of fraudulent behavior.

Regulatory reporting is a cornerstone of compliance, serving as a conduit for transparency between market participants and regulators. Institutions must submit a variety of reports, including financial statements, transaction records, and disclosures of material events. These requirements ensure that regulators have access to critical information necessary for monitoring market activities and enforcing regulations. For example, the Dodd-Frank Act in the United States mandates comprehensive reporting of derivatives transactions to ensure transparency and mitigate systemic risks.

One specific type of regulatory report is the Suspicious Activity Report (SAR), which financial institutions must file when they detect potential cases of money laundering or other suspicious activities. The SAR provides regulators with detailed information about the nature of the suspicious activity, aiding in the investigation and enforcement process. Failure to file a SAR or inadequate reporting can result in severe penalties, emphasizing the importance of thorough and timely compliance.

Compliance with trading and market activities also includes adherence to best execution policies. These policies require brokers and trading firms to execute client orders at the most favorable terms available, considering factors such as price, speed, and likelihood of execution. Best execution is paramount in maintaining market integrity and protecting investor interests, ensuring that market participants receive fair treatment.

The implementation of compliance programs necessitates robust internal controls and regular audits to assess adherence to regulatory requirements. Institutions must conduct periodic reviews of their compliance policies, processes, and risk management systems to identify and rectify any deficiencies. Internal audits, coupled with regulatory examinations, ensure that compliance practices are continuously improved and aligned with evolving regulatory standards.

Technology plays a pivotal role in enhancing compliance processes through automation, data analytics, and real-time monitoring. Advanced software solutions enable institutions to streamline their compliance functions, reduce manual errors, and improve the efficiency of reporting. For instance, automated transaction monitoring systems can analyze vast amounts of data to detect anomalies, generating alerts for further investigation by compliance officers.

The cost of non-compliance can be substantial, encompassing not only financial penalties but also reputational damage and loss of investor confidence. High-profile cases of non-compliance can erode trust in financial markets, prompting stricter regulatory scrutiny and more stringent enforcement actions. Thus, institutions must prioritize their compliance efforts to safeguard their operational legitimacy and maintain investor trust.

Global differences in compliance and reporting requirements pose additional challenges for institutions engaged in cross-border trading. Each jurisdiction may have its own set of regulations, requiring firms to navigate and reconcile varying standards. To mitigate these complexities, firms often rely on global compliance teams and external legal advisors to ensure adherence across multiple regulatory environments.

The dynamic nature of financial markets necessitates continuous advancements in compliance frameworks. With the rise of fintech innovations, regulatory technology (RegTech) has emerged as a significant trend, employing cutting-edge technologies like artificial intelligence and blockchain to enhance regulatory compliance. RegTech solutions offer promising avenues for improving the accuracy, speed, and cost-efficiency of compliance processes, enabling institutions to better manage their regulatory obligations in an ever-evolving landscape.

Through effective compliance and diligent reporting, market participants contribute to the overall health and robustness of the financial ecosystem. By upholding standards of integrity, transparency, and accountability, they foster an environment where investor confidence and market stability can flourish, paving the way for sustainable economic growth.

7.6   Impact of Regulation on Market Behavior

The regulatory landscape plays an indispensable role in shaping the behaviors and dynamics of financial markets. Regulations are designed to ensure fair trading practices, enhance transparency, protect investors, and maintain market integrity. Their impact is multifaceted, influencing how markets operate, how participants interact, and ultimately, market outcomes.

One of the most significant impacts of regulation is on market transparency. By mandating disclosure of certain information, regulations compel market participants to make their trading activities more visible.

This transparency aims to level the playing field, allowing all investors, regardless of size or sophistication, to make informed decisions. Consider, for example, the Securities Exchange Act of 1934, which introduced rules requiring companies to file quarterly and annual reports. Such disclosure regulations help reduce information asymmetry, where some investors might otherwise possess superior information over others. This reduction in asymmetry can lead to more stable and efficient markets, as informed trading decisions are based on a comprehensive view of available information.

Furthermore, regulations directly impact market liquidity. Liquidity—commonly defined as the ability to quickly buy or sell assets without causing significant price changes—is vital for the smooth functioning of markets. Rules like the Volcker Rule, part of the Dodd-Frank Wall Street Reform and Consumer Protection Act, limit proprietary trading by banks, potentially reducing liquidity for certain financial instruments. However, such regulations aim to curb excessive risk-taking and prevent financial crises. Therefore, while there may be short-term impacts on liquidity, the overarching objective is to stabilize markets long-term.

Market behavior is also significantly affected by fraud prevention and enforcement regulations. Anti-fraud provisions, such as those detailed in the Sarbanes-Oxley Act of 2002, seek to deter market manipulation, insider trading, and other unethical practices. These provisions mandate strict penalties for violations, thereby fostering a culture of compliance. An environment where fraudulent practices are minimized enhances investor confidence, encouraging greater participation and investment in the markets. Higher confidence among investors typically results in increased buying and selling activities, contributing to overall market depth and resilience.

The introduction and modification of market regulations can also alter trading strategies, particularly in the realm of algorithmic and high-frequency trading (HFT). For instance, the implementation of Regulation National Market System (Reg NMS) in the United States in 2005 aimed to modernize and strengthen the national market system for equity securities. Reg NMS includes Rule 611, known as the Order Protection Rule, which prevents trade-throughs (executions at inferior prices). This regulation has prompted a reevaluation of trading algorithms to ensure compliance while seeking the most competitive trade executions. By creating a more interconnected and efficient trading environment, Reg NMS fosters competition among trading venues and can reduce transaction costs for investors.

Regulations can further impact cross-border trading and international market behavior. Different regulatory standards between countries can create arbitrage opportunities but also pose compliance challenges for global investors. Harmonizing international regulations, as seen with the adoption of the Markets in Financial Instruments Directive (MiFID II) in the European Union, seeks to create a more level playing field across different jurisdictions. MiFID II enhances market transparency and investor protection, impacting not only European markets but also global entities trading within the EU. Consequently, firms are required to adjust their operations to comply with these enhanced standards, often leading to significant shifts in trading practices and market strategies.

In addition to these specific examples, the broader impact of regulation on market behavior is evident in market participants' increased focus on compliance and risk management. Regulations mandating robust compliance programs and regular auditing encourage firms to adopt rigorous internal controls. This shift towards greater prudence and accountability helps mitigate systemic risks, contributing to market stability even during volatile periods.

Ultimately, while regulations can introduce certain constraints on market operations and trading behaviors, they are instrumental in fostering a stable, transparent, and fair trading environment. The balancing act between regulatory oversight and market freedom continues to evolve, aiming to adapt to new financial innovations and emerging risks while preserving market integrity. As regulations evolve, they will invariably shape market behavior in ways that promote long-term sustainability and investor confidence.

7.7   Global Differences in Market Regulation

Understanding the nuances of market regulation across different geographies is essential for traders and investors operating in global markets. Regulations vary significantly, impacting everything from trading hours and reporting requirements to the types of instruments that can be traded. These differences can influence trading strategies, market behavior, and even the overall efficiency of capital markets. In this section, we delve into the primary differences in market regulations across major financial centers, highlighting their implications for market participants.

The United States, for instance, operates under a highly structured regulatory framework. The primary regulatory bodies include the Securities and Exchange Commission (SEC) and the Commodity Futures Trading Commission (CFTC). The SEC oversees securities markets, enforcing rigorous disclosure requirements to enhance transparency and protect investors. Financial markets in the U.S. also adhere to the Sarbanes-Oxley Act, which imposes strict regulations on corporate governance and financial practices, particularly for public companies. This regulatory environment, while stringent, aims to foster investor confidence and market integrity.

In contrast, European markets operate under a different set of regulatory standards, primarily guided by the European Securities and Markets Authority (ESMA) and individual national regulators. The Markets in Financial Instruments Directive II (MiFID II) and the Market Abuse Regulation (MAR) are cornerstone legislations in this region. MiFID II, implemented in 2018, revolutionized market operations by enhancing transparency, bolstering investor protection, and encouraging competition among trading venues. Unlike the United States, European regulations place a stronger emphasis on safeguarding the interests of smaller investors, given the region's diverse financial landscape.

Asian markets, encompassing hubs like Tokyo, Singapore, and Hong Kong, present yet another regulatory paradigm. Japan's Financial Services Agency (FSA) supervises its financial markets with an intricate blend of rules promoting transparency and protection. Notably, the Tokyo Stock Exchange mandates rigorous compliance for listed companies, emphasizing timely and accurate disclosures. Comparatively, in Hong Kong, the Securities and Futures Commission (SFC) regulates with a framework designed to uphold market integrity and robustness, often balancing between stringent supervision and fostering business growth. Singapore, regulated by the Monetary Authority of Singapore (MAS), is renowned for its progressive and adaptive regulatory environment, attracting a myriad of financial institutions and fostering innovation in financial products and services.

These variations in regulation also impact algorithmic trading and high-frequency trading (HFT) practices. For example, while the United States allows relatively liberal conditions for HFT, underpinned by its sophisticated technology infrastructure, Europe imposes stricter controls to mitigate risks associated with market abuse and instability. MiFID II, for instance, introduced comprehensive rules for algorithmic trading, mandating registration, monitoring, and testing of trading algorithms. Asian markets, being diverse, reflect a mix of these approaches, with varying levels of regulatory oversight and technological advancement.

The implications of these regulatory differences are profound for market participants. Traders and investors must adapt their strategies to align with local regulations, affecting everything from order execution to portfolio management. For instance, the stringent disclosure requirements in the United States lead to a wealth of publicly available information, enabling data-driven investment strategies. Conversely, the focus on investor protection in Europe might necessitate more conservative trading approaches, especially for retail investors.

Cross-border trading also faces regulatory challenges. Differences in trading hours, settlement cycles, and reporting standards can complicate international transactions. For example, while U.S. markets operate on T+2 (trade date plus two days) settlement cycle, some European markets still operate on T+2 or even T+3. Such discrepancies necessitate sophisticated risk management systems to handle settlement risk, especially in volatile market conditions.

The global regulatory landscape is continually evolving, driven by technological advancements, market innovations, and economic shifts. For instance, the rise of cryptocurrencies and blockchain technology has prompted regulatory bodies worldwide to adapt and create frameworks to oversee these emerging assets. The European Union's proposed Markets in Crypto-Assets (MiCA) regulation is a case in point, aiming to establish a regulatory framework for cryptocurrency markets across Europe, while the U.S. and Asian regulators are still in varied stages of developing similar regulations.

Understanding these differences and their ongoing evolution is crucial for effective compliance and strategic planning. Traders and investors who navigate these complexities successfully can leverage regulatory arbitrage opportunities, optimize their trading operations, and achieve better risk-adjusted returns. As globalization deepens, staying attuned to regulatory changes across different markets will be paramount for maintaining competitive edge and ensuring sustainable growth in global trading and investment activities.

Market regulation, while often seen as a constraint, is fundamentally designed to protect market integrity, promote transparency, and foster investor confidence. By appreciating the unique regulatory frameworks of various global markets, market participants can better navigate the complexities of international trading, ultimately contributing to more efficient and stable financial systems.

Chapter 8

Algorithmic Trading Strategies

This chapter covers the fundamentals of algorithmic trading, detailing various types of algorithmic strategies used in financial markets. It explores specific strategies such as market making, trend following, and statistical arbitrage, explaining their mechanics and objectives. The chapter also delves into execution algorithms designed to optimize trade execution and minimize market impact. Practical aspects of building and testing algorithmic strategies are discussed, providing insights into the development and refinement of effective automated trading systems.

8.1   Basics of Algorithmic Trading

Algorithmic trading, often referred to as algo trading, employs computer algorithms to automate the process of trading financial assets. These algorithms can execute trades at speeds and frequencies that are beyond the capacity of human traders, analyzing vast datasets to identify and exploit trading opportunities in real-time.

The development of algorithmic trading has significantly transformed the landscape of financial markets, offering both profound benefits and notable challenges. To fully grasp the basics of algorithmic trading, we must explore its fundamental components, advantages, potential risks, and the key terminologies essential for understanding this field.

At its core, algorithmic trading relies on a set of predefined rules and instructions that a computer program follows to place trades. These rules can be as simple or as complex as needed, ranging from executing trades based on basic moving average crossovers to implementing sophisticated statistical models that analyze multiple market conditions simultaneously.

Market efficiency is one of the primary motivations behind the adoption of algorithmic trading. By leveraging powerful computing capabilities, algorithms can reduce the market impact of trades, enhance liquidity provisioning, and overall improve the market's efficiency. However, this requires a nuanced understanding of both market microstructure and the algorithms themselves.

Key Components of Algorithmic Trading Systems

The architecture of an algorithmic trading system generally consists of several critical components:

- **Data Acquisition:** High-quality and timely data is paramount. This includes market data such as prices, volumes, and order book depth, as well as alternative data sources like social media sentiment or macroeconomic indicators.

- **Trading Algorithms:** These are the heart of the system, incorporating various strategies to make trading decisions. Algorithms may include technical indicators, pattern recognition systems, or advanced quantitative models based on statistical and mathematical theories.

- **Execution Engine:** This component implements the trading decisions made by the algorithms. It is responsible for placing orders in the market while optimizing for factors like latency, slippage, and transaction costs.

- **Risk Management:** Effective risk management frameworks are crucial to safeguard capital and ensure the longevity of the trading strategy. These include position sizing rules, portfolio diversification, stop-loss mechanisms, and stress testing under adverse market conditions.

- **Compliance and Monitoring:** Even automated systems must comply with regulatory requirements and internal policies. Real-time monitoring tools help in detecting anomalies and ensuring that the system operates within set parameters.

Advantages of Algorithmic Trading

The adoption of algorithmic trading offers numerous advantages:

- **Speed and Efficiency:** Algorithms can execute trades in milliseconds, capitalizing on the smallest price inefficiencies that are often short-lived.

- **Consistency:** Algorithms operate without the influence of emotions, adhering strictly to predefined rules. This removes the risk of emotional trading decisions that can lead to inconsistent performance.

- **Scalability:** Once developed, an algorithm can be scaled to trade across multiple assets and markets, enabling a diversified approach that would be challenging to achieve manually.

- **Backtesting and Optimization:** Algorithms can be rigorously tested on historical data to validate their effectiveness before being deployed in live markets. This allows for continuous improvement through iterative refinement.

- **Cost Efficiency:** By minimizing the necessity for human intervention, firms can reduce operational costs associated with trading activities.

Potential Risks and Challenges

While algorithmic trading offers numerous benefits, it also presents certain risks and challenges that need to be meticulously managed:

- **Model Risk:** The reliance on mathematical models exposes traders to the risk of model errors, which can lead to significant financial losses.

- **Systemic Risk:** The interconnected nature of automated trading systems can amplify market volatility, as witnessed during events like the Flash Crash of 2010.

- **Technical Failures:** Hardware malfunctions, software bugs, and connectivity issues can disrupt trading operations, often with costly consequences.

- **Regulatory Risk:** Financial markets are heavily regulated, and compliance with evolving regulatory standards is essential to avoid legal and financial penalties.

Key Terminologies in Algorithmic Trading

Understanding basic terminologies is crucial for anyone venturing into the domain of algorithmic trading:

- **Latency:** The time delay between the initiation of a trading signal and the execution of the trade. Lower latency is often crucial for the success of high-frequency trading strategies.

- **Alpha:** The excess return of an investment relative to a benchmark index. In the context of algorithmic trading, alpha refers to the profitability potential of a trading strategy.

- **Slippage:** The difference between the expected price of a trade and the actual executed price. Slippage can significantly impact the profitability of high-frequency trading strategies.

- **Backtesting:** The process of testing a trading strategy on historical data to evaluate its effectiveness. Effective backtesting frameworks are integral to the development of reliable trading algorithms.

- **Execution Algorithm:** Algorithms designed specifically to optimize the execution of trades, minimizing market impact and transaction costs.

With a solid understanding of the basics of algorithmic trading, readers are better equipped to delve into specific algorithmic strategies. These strategies form the backbone of modern algorithmic trading systems and are tailored to exploit various market inefficiencies and trends. The subsequent sections will explore these strategies in greater detail, providing insight into their mechanics and applications.

8.2   Types of Algorithmic Strategies

Algorithmic trading strategies are diverse, each finely tuned to exploit specific market inefficiencies or dynamics. Understanding the different types of algorithmic strategies is crucial for developing a robust and adaptive trading approach. This section will delve into the primary categories of algorithmic strategies, outlining their mechanics, objectives, and typical implementation considerations.

Algorithmic strategies can be broadly classified into two categories: directional and non-directional strategies. Directional strategies predict the direction of price movements, while non-directional strategies seek to profit from relative price movements or inefficiencies without necessarily predicting the overall market direction. Let's examine these strategies in more detail.

Directional strategies include momentum and trend-following algorithms. These strategies capitalize on the persistence of price trends or momentum, assuming that assets exhibiting strong performance will continue to do so in the short to medium term. To identify and exploit these trends, technical indicators such as moving averages, relative strength index (RSI), and MACD (Moving Average Convergence Divergence) are often employed. For instance, a simple moving average cross-over strategy might buy an asset when a short-term moving average crosses above a long-term moving average, signaling upward momentum.

While momentum strategies focus on the continuation of trends, mean reversion strategies operate on the opposite principle: the expectation that prices will revert to their historical average. Mean reversion algorithms often use statistical measures like standard deviation and mean to identify overbought or oversold conditions. When an asset's price deviates significantly from its average value, trading signals are generated to exploit the anticipated price correction. A classical mean reversion strategy might involve Bollinger Bands, where buying occurs when the price touches the lower band and selling ensues when it reaches the upper band.

Arbitrage strategies are a prominent non-directional category. These strategies exploit price discrepancies between related securities or markets. One common form is statistical arbitrage, which relies on historical price relationships and quantitative models to identify mispricings. A pair trading strategy, where traders buy an undervalued security and simultaneously sell a related overvalued security, is a typical example. The profit is achieved when prices converge. Another variant is index arbitrage, which capitalizes on the price differences between index futures and their constituent stocks.

Market making algorithms, another significant non-directional strategy, enhance market liquidity by continuously quoting both buy (bid) and sell (ask) prices for a security. These algorithms profit from the bid-ask spread, the difference between buy and sell prices. Effective market making requires sophisticated modeling to dynamically adjust quotes in response to market conditions, inventory levels, and order flow.

Execution algorithms, such as VWAP (Volume Weighted Average Price) and TWAP (Time Weighted Average Price), optimize trade execution by minimizing the market impact and transaction costs. These strategies break large orders into smaller pieces and execute them over time, following specific benchmarks. VWAP strategies seek to execute an order at the average price weighted by volume over a specific period, often used by institutional investors to avoid moving the market price unfavorably during large trades.

Finally, high-frequency trading (HFT) strategies operate at extreme speeds, executing trades within milliseconds. HFT leverages advanced technology and co-location services to gain proximity to exchanges, minimizing latency. These strategies often employ elements of market making, arbitrage, and statistical models to capture fleeting opportunities in market data. HFT requires substantial investment in infrastructure and risk management to maintain a competitive edge and adhere to regulatory standards.

Each type of algorithmic strategy requires specialized knowledge and tools for effective implementation. Understanding the underlying principles, market conditions, and risk factors associated with each strategy is fundamental to developing a successful algorithmic trading approach. As we progress through this chapter, these concepts will be further enriched with practical insights into building and testing these sophisticated strategies.

8.3 Market Making Algorithms

Market-making algorithms form an essential part of the financial markets, facilitating liquidity and providing smoother price discovery mechanisms. Understanding the intricacies of market making algorithms enables traders to comprehend how liquidity providers operate and how these algorithms influence market dynamics.

Market making involves simultaneously quoting buy (bid) and sell (ask) prices for a security or derivative, aiming to profit from the spread between these quotes while managing the inventory risk. This section elucidates the core principles and practical implementations of market-making algorithms, addressing their mechanisms, objectives, and the challenges faced in dynamic market environments.

At its core, a market maker seeks to capitalize on the bid-ask spread by providing quotes on both sides of the order book. The fundamental objective is to earn profits through frequent, small gains from the spread while mitigating the exposure to adverse price movements. Efficient market making algorithms are designed to balance the trade-off between providing liquidity and managing inventory risk.

To illustrate these concepts rigorously, consider the following notations and variables:

$P_b(t) =$ Bid price at time t,

$P_a(t) =$ Ask price at time t,

$S = P_a(t) - P_b(t) =$ Bid-ask spread,

$q_i =$ Inventory position of the market maker at time t.

A successful market making strategy necessitates algorithms capable of dynamically adjusting bid and ask prices in response to varying market conditions. Key components of these algorithms include:

- **Price Quoting Models:** Central to the market-making process is the continuous adjustment of price quotes. Common quoting models involve:

  - a. *Static Quoting:* Fixed bid-ask spreads are maintained regardless of market fluctuations. Although simple, this method is prone to higher inventory risk during volatile periods.

  - b. *Dynamic Quoting:* Adjusts the bid-ask spread based on real-time volatility and order flow. Dynamic quoting ensures competitive pricing, reducing the likelihood of adverse selection and mitigating inventory risk.

$$P_b(t) = \max\left(P_m(t) - \frac{S}{2}, \text{threshold}_b \right),$$

$$P_a(t) = \min\left(P_m(t) + \frac{S}{2}, \text{threshold}_a \right),$$

where $P_m(t)$ is the mid-price and threshold_b, threshold_a signify boundaries set for bid and ask prices respectively.

- **Inventory Management:** Effective inventory management is crucial for market makers to remain profitable. The primary strategies include:

  - *a. Mean Reversion:* Centers on the premise that asset prices oscillate around a long-term mean. Inventory imbalance is managed by adjusting prices to encourage trades that offset the imbalance.

  $$q_i = \beta(P_m(t) - P_{ref}) + \epsilon,$$

  where β represents sensitivity to price movements and P_{ref} denotes the reference price around which the mean reversion occurs.

  - *b. Risk Aversion:* Implements risk limits to control exposure, ensuring the market maker does not hold positions that exceed predefined thresholds. Positions are adjusted to minimize the risk of substantial adverse price movements.

  $$q_{target} = -\gamma \left(q_i - q_{opt}\right),$$

  with γ representing the adjustment sensitivity and q_{opt} being the optimal inventory level.

- **Order Execution:** Efficient execution of quoted prices enhances the probability of transaction completion while minimizing market impact. Techniques include:

  - *a. Optimal Execution:* Balances order size and execution speed to achieve the best market impact cost over a given time horizon.

  $$O_{exec} = \alpha q_i + (1 - \alpha) \left(\frac{v_m(t)}{V_t}\right),$$

  where α indicates the weight of inventory versus market volume considerations, $v_m(t)$ is the market volume, and V_t total intended volume to trade.

  - *b. Hidden Orders:* Utilize non-displayed limit orders to avoid revealing the market maker's true intentions, providing an edge in execution without impacting the visible order book.

Market making algorithms also integrate advanced statistical methods and real-time data analytics. By employing machine learning models and predictive analytics, market makers can forecast short-term price movements and adapt their strategies accordingly. These models analyze patterns in market data, such as order flow and trade volume, to enhance decision-making processes and improve pricing accuracy.

Given the complexities and fast-paced nature of modern financial markets, it is imperative for market makers to continuously refine their algorithms. This involves rigorous backtesting using historical data to validate the strategies, along with stress testing under various market scenarios to ensure robustness and adaptability.

Ultimately, mastering market-making algorithms requires a blend of theoretical knowledge and practical experimentation. By understanding the principles outlined in this section, traders and algorithm developers can gain valuable insights into the mechanics of market making, enabling the design and implementation of sophisticated and resilient trading strategies.

8.4 Trend Following Algorithms

Trend following algorithms are an essential class of strategies within the realm of algorithmic trading. These strategies capitalize on market momentum, systematically capturing profits by identifying and exploiting enduring trends in asset prices. Trend following is rooted in the belief that markets often exhibit extended periods of directional movement, both upward and downward, due to the collective actions of market participants.

At its core, trend following is predicated on the assumption that once a trend is established, it is more likely to continue than reverse. This section explores the fundamental principles of trend following, the various techniques used to identify trends, and practical considerations for implementing and testing trend-following algorithms.

Fundamental Principles of Trend Following

Trend following relies on a few key principles:

- **Price is the Primary Signal**: The approach is purely technical, focusing on price movements rather than fundamental data. Historical price data, moving averages, and other trend indicators are the primary tools.

- **Risk Management**: Successful trend following requires strict risk management to protect capital and maximize returns during trending periods.

- **Diversification**: Trend followers often diversify across various markets and asset classes to spread risk and increase the probability of capturing trends.

Techniques for Identifying Trends

Several methods are commonly employed to detect trends within financial data:

- **Moving Averages**: Moving averages smooth out price data to identify the direction of the trend. A simple moving average (SMA) or an exponential moving average (EMA) can be used. For instance, a popular approach is the moving average crossover, where a short-term moving average crossing above a long-term moving average signals a potential upward trend, and vice versa.

$$\text{SMA}_n = \frac{1}{n} \sum_{i=0}^{n-1} P_{t-i}$$

- **Breakout Systems**: Breakout strategies involve entering positions when the price surpasses historical high or low levels, indicating a potential new trend. This method bets on the notion that significant price moves often follow such breakouts.

$$\text{Long Entry: } P_t > \max(P_{t-n}, \ldots, P_{t-1})$$
$$\text{Short Entry: } P_t < \min(P_{t-n}, \ldots, P_{t-1})$$

- **Relative Strength Index (RSI)**: The RSI is a momentum oscillator that measures the speed and change of price movements. It can help identify potential trend reversals and confirm existing trends. An RSI above 70 typically indicates overbought conditions, while an RSI below 30 indicates oversold conditions.

$$\text{RSI}_n = 100 - \left(\frac{100}{1 + \frac{\text{Average Gain}}{\text{Average Loss}}} \right)$$

Implementation of Trend Following Algorithms

- **Entry and Exit Signals**: Establish clear entry and exit rules based on trend indicators. For example, a moving average crossover system might generate an entry signal when the 50-day SMA crosses above the 200-day SMA and an exit when the reverse occurs.

```
if short_term_sma > long_term_sma:
    buy()
elif short_term_sma < long_term_sma:
    sell()
```

- **Position Sizing**: Determine the size of positions based on account equity and risk tolerance. Techniques such as volatility-adjusted position sizing, where position size is adjusted based on the asset's volatility, can be effective in managing risk.

$$\text{Position Size} = \frac{\text{Risk Capital}}{\text{Stop Loss Distance} \times ATR}$$

- **Risk Management**: Implement stop losses and trailing stops to protect against significant drawdowns. Setting a maximum loss threshold for each trade based on a percentage of account equity is a common practice.

$$\text{Stop Loss} = \text{Entry Price} - (\text{Risk} \times \text{ATR})$$

Practical Considerations

- **Backtesting**: Conduct thorough backtesting using historical data to evaluate the performance and robustness of the trend-following strategy. Key metrics to assess include the Sharpe ratio, maximum drawdown, and overall profitability.

$$\text{Sharpe Ratio} = \frac{E[R_p - R_f]}{\sigma_p}$$

- **Parameter Optimization**: Trend following strategies often involve parameters that can significantly impact performance, such as the period of moving averages or the breakout threshold. Optimization techniques, such as walk-forward analysis and cross-validation, can help identify robust parameter settings.

133

- **Market Adaptation**: Trends can vary greatly across different markets and timeframes. It is crucial to periodically re-evaluate and adjust the strategy to adapt to changing market conditions. This could involve altering indicator parameters or incorporating new data sources.

- **Diversification and Correlation**: To mitigate the risk of market-specific events adversely affecting the trading strategy, diversify across multiple markets and asset classes. Analyzing the correlation between assets can help in constructing a diversified portfolio.

By adhering to these principles and considerations, traders can leverage trend following algorithms to harness market momentum effectively. The simplicity and systematic nature of trend following make it an enduring and widely used strategy in algorithmic trading portfolios. As we proceed to explore the complexities of other algorithms, understanding the foundational approaches like trend following will provide a solid base for more advanced methodologies.

8.5 Statistical Arbitrage

Statistical arbitrage, often referred to as *stat arb*, is a sophisticated trading strategy that involves the simultaneous buying and selling of two or more securities to exploit pricing inefficiencies between them. This strategy relies heavily on statistical and mathematical models to identify opportunities where the prices of related assets are deviating from their expected relationship. The key to successful statistical arbitrage lies in data analysis, superior modeling techniques, and robust risk management.

The foundation of statistical arbitrage is the notion that prices of certain securities are co-integrated, meaning they have a stable, long-term relationship. When the prices deviate from this equilibrium, a mean-reversion process is expected, allowing traders to profit from the convergence. This approach is particularly prevalent in pairs trading, a common form of stat arb, where a trader simultaneously goes long on an undervalued security and short on an overvalued one, anticipating that their prices will revert to the mean.

To illustrate, consider two stocks, X and Y, which historically exhibit co-integration. Suppose an analysis reveals that the ratio of their prices,

$Z = \frac{P_X}{P_Y}$, fluctuates around a mean value μ with a standard deviation σ. When Z diverges significantly from μ, a trading opportunity emerges. If Z is much higher than μ, a trader might short X and go long Y, expecting Z to decrease towards μ. Conversely, if Z is much lower than μ, the trader would go long X and short Y, anticipating an increase in Z.

Mathematically, the trading signal S can be represented as:

$$S = Z - \mu$$

When $|S|$ exceeds a predefined threshold $K \times \sigma$, where K is a constant chosen based on the trader's risk tolerance and statistical confidence, a trade is triggered. This approach capitalizes on mean reversion, assuming the spread will contract over time.

Implementing statistical arbitrage involves several steps:

- **Data Collection and Preparation**: Historical price data for the securities under consideration must be gathered and cleaned. This involves ensuring data quality and adjusting for corporate actions like dividends, stock splits, and mergers.

- **Statistical Analysis and Model Building**: Employing statistical techniques such as regression analysis and time-series modeling, traders identify co-integrated pairs. Methods like the Engle-Granger two-step approach or the Johansen test are commonly used to test for co-integration.

- **Backtesting**: The developed model is rigorously tested using historical data to evaluate its performance. Backtesting helps in understanding the model's behavior under various market conditions, identifying potential weaknesses, and optimizing parameters.

- **Risk Management**: Effective risk management strategies are crucial. Traders must define stop-loss limits, position sizing rules, and manage exposure to market, execution, and operational risks. Employing techniques like dynamic hedging and portfolio diversification can help mitigate risks.

- **Execution**: Once a trading opportunity is identified, the execution strategy must minimize market impact and transaction costs. Execution algorithms such as VWAP (Volume Weighted Average Price) or TWAP (Time Weighted Average Price) can be employed to achieve this.

- **Monitoring and Refinement**: Continuous monitoring of active trades and periodic review of the model's performance are essential. Market conditions change, and models may drift from their original assumptions. Adaptive algorithms and machine learning techniques can help keep the strategies up-to-date and robust.

To underscore the statistical rigor involved, consider the pair trading example where the spread Z follows a normal distribution $N(\mu, \sigma^2)$. The probability of $|S|$ exceeding a certain level can be calculated using the normal distribution's cumulative density function (CDF):

$$P(|S| > K \cdot \sigma) = 2\left(1 - \Phi(K)\right)$$

where Φ is the CDF of a standard normal distribution. This probability informs the trader about the likelihood of a significant deviation and helps in setting an appropriate threshold K.

Although statistical arbitrage can be highly profitable, it carries risks. Model assumptions may break down during periods of market stress, liquidity constraints can exacerbate losses, and the strategy's profitability can be eroded by competition as others exploit similar inefficiencies. Thus, constant vigilance, model refinement, and robust risk management are imperative for success in statistical arbitrage.

This integration of statistical analysis, algorithmic execution, and risk management underpins the sophisticated nature of statistical arbitrage, distinguishing it as a powerful yet complex trading strategy in modern financial markets.

8.6 Execution Algorithms

Execution algorithms are designed to facilitate the efficient execution of large orders in financial markets, minimizing market impact and achieving the best possible prices. These algorithms are particularly crucial for institutional investors and large traders who need to buy or sell substantial quantities of assets without significantly moving the market. In this section, we will examine the primary types of execution algorithms, their objectives, and the methodologies they employ.

Execution algorithms can be broadly categorized into two primary types: volume-based algorithms and time-based algorithms. Each has its specific set of strategies and techniques tailored to achieve optimal execution performance.

Volume-based algorithms aim to execute orders in proportion to the market's trading volume. One of the most prominent volume-based algorithms is the Volume-Weighted Average Price (VWAP) algorithm. The VWAP algorithm divides the total order into smaller slices and executes these slices based on the historical or real-time volume profile of the market. The goal is to achieve an average execution price that is close to the VWAP benchmark, representing a fair price relative to market volume. Mathematically, the VWAP is defined as:

$$\text{VWAP} = \frac{\sum_{i=1}^{n} P_i \cdot Q_i}{\sum_{i=1}^{n} Q_i}$$

where P_i is the price of the i-th trade, Q_i is the quantity of the i-th trade, and n is the total number of trades during the period.

Another notable volume-based algorithm is the Participation Rate (PoV, or Percentage of Volume) algorithm, which aims to participate in trading at a given rate of total market volume. The PoV algorithm dynamically adjusts the order size according to the real-time trading volume, ensuring that the trader does not exceed the pre-set participation rate. By doing so, it minimizes the market impact and conforms to the natural liquidity of the market.

Time-based algorithms, on the other hand, focus on executing orders within a specified time frame, regardless of the market volume. One common time-based algorithm is the Time-Weighted Average Price (TWAP) algorithm. The TWAP algorithm breaks down the order into equally sized slices and executes them at regular intervals over the specified period. This approach is beneficial when a trader aims to distribute their market presence evenly over time, avoiding large price swings that could result from concentrated market activity.

$$\text{TWAP} = \frac{1}{T} \sum_{t=1}^{T} P_t$$

where P_t is the execution price at time t, and T represents the total number of time intervals.

A more sophisticated approach combining both volume and time elements is the Implementation Shortfall algorithm. This algorithm aims to minimize the total cost of executing an order, inclusive of both explicit costs (e.g., commissions) and implicit costs (e.g., market impact and opportunity cost). The implementation shortfall is calculated as the difference between the execution price and the initial decision price, accounting for market conditions and order size. This technique leverages complex models to balance the trade-off between executing swiftly (minimizing opportunity costs) and minimizing market impact by executing gradually.

$$\text{Implementation Shortfall} = (P_\text{execution} - P_\text{decision}) \times Q + \text{Commissions}$$

where $P_{execution}$ is the average execution price, $P_{decision}$ is the decision price when the order was initiated, and Q is the total quantity of the order.

Selecting the appropriate execution algorithm involves understanding the specific requirements of the trade and the characteristics of the market. Factors such as market liquidity, volatility, order size, and time constraints must be carefully considered. Advanced execution algorithms often incorporate machine learning and real-time market data analysis to adaptively adjust their strategies, thereby optimizing execution performance in dynamic market conditions.

Execution algorithms play a pivotal role in modern trading, enabling large orders to be executed with minimal adverse effects on the market. By understanding and effectively utilizing these algorithms, traders can significantly enhance their execution efficiency, achieving better prices and reducing trading costs. As markets continue to evolve, the ongoing development of more advanced and adaptive execution algorithms will remain a critical area of focus for trading technology and financial engineering.

8.7   Building and Testing Algorithmic Strategies

Building and testing algorithmic strategies is a critical component of successful algorithmic trading. This process involves several stages, each crucial for the development of a robust and profitable trading system. Understanding and mastering these stages allow both novice and experienced traders to design systems that maximize returns while minimizing risks.

The first step in building an algorithmic strategy is idea generation. This involves conceptualizing a potential trading strategy based on market observations, historical patterns, or theoretical models. For example, one might observe that certain stocks exhibit momentum following earnings announcements, suggesting a trend-following strategy. This idea should be framed into a hypothesis that can be systematically tested.

Once an idea has been generated, it must be formalized into a set of rules. These rules define the strategy's entry and exit signals, the conditions under which trades are executed, and any constraints or risk management techniques to be employed. A typical momentum strategy might involve buying stocks that have shown significant price appreciation over a specific period and selling them when they begin to show signs of reversal. The key is to ensure that these rules are clear, unambiguous, and implementable using a computer algorithm.

Next, the strategy must be coded into an executable algorithm. This step requires a solid understanding of programming and the trading platform's infrastructure. Several programming languages are popular in the trading community, including Python, C++, and Java. Python is particularly favored for its readability and the extensive libraries available for data analysis and financial modeling. Below is a sample Python snippet to illustrate the coding of a simple moving average crossover strategy:

```python
import pandas as pd

def moving_average_crossover(data, short_window, long_window):
    # Calculate moving averages
    signals = pd.DataFrame(index=data.index)
    signals['price'] = data['close']
    signals['short_mavg'] = data['close'].rolling(window=short_window).mean()
    signals['long_mavg'] = data['close'].rolling(window=long_window).mean()

    # Generate signals
    signals['signal'] = 0
    signals['signal'][short_window:] = np.where(signals['short_mavg'][short_window:] >
        signals['long_mavg'][short_window:], 1, 0)
    signals['positions'] = signals['signal'].diff()

    return signals
```

Once coded, the strategy moves into the backtesting phase. Backtesting involves applying the algorithm to historical market data to see how it would have performed in the past. This step helps to identify potential flaws or weaknesses in the strategy and provides a preliminary assessment of its profitability. It is imperative to use high-quality historical data and account for all trading costs, including commissions and slippage.

An important aspect of backtesting is the need to avoid overfitting. Overfitting occurs when a model becomes too closely tailored to historical data, capturing noise rather than genuine patterns. Strategies that overfit historical data often perform poorly in live trading. To mitigate this risk, traders should employ out-of-sample testing, where the data is divided into two sets: one for training the model and one for testing its performance on unseen data.

Additionally, walk-forward optimization can be used to dynamically adapt the strategy parameters. This approach involves dividing historical data into multiple segments and optimizing the model on each segment iteratively, effectively simulating a changing market environment.

After successful backtesting, the strategy should be tested in a simulated live environment. This stage, often called paper trading, involves executing the algorithm in real-time on live market data without actual financial risk. Paper trading helps to identify practical issues such as latency, data feed errors, and unexpected behavior under live market conditions.

For a comprehensive evaluation, the strategy's performance metrics must be meticulously analyzed. Key metrics include the following:

- **Sharpe Ratio:** A measure of risk-adjusted return.

- **Max Drawdown:** The maximum loss from peak to trough.

- **Profit Factor:** The ratio of gross profit to gross loss.

- **Win Rate:** The percentage of profitable trades.

If the strategy performs well during these tests, it may be deployed with actual capital. However, even at this stage, continuous monitoring and periodic re-evaluation are essential. Markets evolve, and a strategy that works today may not work tomorrow. Continual improvement, incorporating new data and adapting to market changes, is critical for long-term success.

By following these steps, traders can develop and refine algorithmic strategies that are both robust and adaptive, positioning themselves to effectively navigate the complex landscape of financial markets.

Chapter 9

Market Design and Efficiency

This chapter examines the principles of market design, exploring different market structures and their impact on efficiency. It discusses the role of auctions, comparing continuous and discrete markets, and evaluates methods for measuring market efficiency. The chapter also investigates common market failures and inefficiencies, proposing design improvements to enhance overall market functioning. Key insights into how strategic market design can foster more effective and equitable trading environments are provided.

9.1 Principles of Market Design

Market design is a critical field that delves into how markets are structured, organized, and regulated to achieve desired economic and social outcomes. Central to market design is the harmonization of interests among various market participants, which includes buyers, sellers, intermediaries, and regulators. Below, we unpack the fundamental principles of market design, shedding light on how these principles contribute to market efficiency and efficacy.

At the heart of market design lies the principle of *allocative efficiency*. This entails creating market conditions wherein resources are distributed in the most valuable manner. Allocative efficiency is achieved when goods and services are allocated to those who value them the most, which typically warrants the use of price mechanisms as signals for scarcity and preference. When markets are well-designed, prices reflect true consumer preferences and producer costs, leading to an optimal allocation of resources.

Another pivotal principle is *price discovery*. Proper market design facilitates the efficient discovery of prices through the interaction of supply and demand. This process ensures that prices carry meaningful information about the underlying value of assets. A well-structured market provides transparency, enabling participants to gauge the market's valuation of different assets accurately. This transparency is essential for reducing information asymmetry where one party has more or better information compared to another.

Markets must also be *liquid*, allowing participants to buy and sell assets with minimal price impact and within a reasonable timeframe. Liquidity is fostered through the presence of market makers, frequent trading, low transaction costs, and tight bid-ask spreads. Careful market design ensures these factors are in place, aiding continuous trading and smooth market operation. For instance, a market with high liquidity provides opportunities for participants to execute large trades without significantly affecting prices, thus preserving market stability.

Another cornerstone in market design is *fairness*, which is achieved through providing equal access to market opportunities and maintaining an even playing field. Fair markets do not allow for manipulation by any participant and have regulations in place to prevent fraud and insider trading. Designing such a market involves creating robust legal and regulatory frameworks that protect market integrity and foster trust among participants. The goal is to ensure that everyone adheres to the same rules and has equal opportunity to compete.

The principle of *risk management* is paramount in market design. Markets must be able to address and mitigate risks stemming from volatility, credit defaults, and systemic failures. Methods such as margin requirements, circuit breakers, and clearinghouses are designed to manage and neutralize such risks. Effective risk management mechanisms enhance market stability and protect participants from disproportionate losses, which can have broader economic repercussions.

Interconnectivity is another important factor. In modern financial markets characterized by complex interdependencies, isolated markets are rare. Efficient market design considers the linkages between different markets, facilitating seamless interactions and transactions across various platforms and jurisdictions. Interconnectivity helps in spreading and managing risks, promoting arbitrage opportunities, and ensuring that price signals in one market reflect global conditions.

Innovation is the dynamic principle that infuses adaptability into market design. Markets must evolve to accommodate technological advances and emerging financial instruments. Regulatory frameworks and market structures should be flexible enough to adapt to innovations such as algorithmic trading, blockchain technology, and decentralized finance (DeFi). An example of innovation in market design is the advent of electronic trading platforms, which have revolutionized trading by increasing speed, reducing costs, and enhancing transparency.

A holistic market design should also consider the *welfare of society* as a whole, ensuring that markets contribute positively to economic and social well-being. This principle calls for a balanced approach where market outcomes do not disproportionately favor certain groups over others. Moreover, ethical considerations, corporate governance, and social responsibility are integrated into the market framework, promoting sustainable and inclusive economic growth.

By adhering to these principles, market designers create environments where efficiency, fairness, and resilience can thrive. The interplay of these principles determines the overall health of a market, guiding its participants towards informed, equitable, and secure trading practices. These foundational concepts set the stage for the more specific topics covered in subsequent sections of this chapter, allowing us to delve deeper into types of market structures, auctions, and strategies for enhancing market efficiency.

9.2 Types of Market Structures and Their Efficiency

Understanding the various types of market structures is pivotal to comprehending how markets function and how they can be optimized for efficiency. Market structures fundamentally define the environment in which buyers and sellers interact, and each type has distinct characteristics that influence trading, liquidity, and price discovery. This section delves into the predominant market structures, analyzing their defining features and their implications for market efficiency.

Market structures are broadly classified into four categories: perfectly competitive markets, monopolistic competition, oligopoly, and monopoly. Each of these market structures presents unique dynamics that affect trade interactions and market performance.

Perfectly Competitive Markets

In a perfectly competitive market, numerous buyers and sellers operate such that no single entity can influence the market price. Key characteristics include homogenous products, free entry and exit, and complete transparency of information. Efficiency in perfectly competitive markets is often high due to the equilibrium between supply and demand prices. Prices tend to reflect the true value of goods or services, and the allocation of resources is generally optimal. However, real-world markets rarely achieve perfect competition due to barriers to entry, product differentiation, and informational asymmetries.

Monopolistic Competition

Monopolistic competition, a more common market structure, involves many firms offering products that are similar but not identical. Differentiation might be based on quality, branding, or other factors that create consumer preference. In this scenario, firms have some degree of price-setting power, which can lead to inefficiencies. While consumer choice is enhanced, the presence of many sellers often results in duplicated efforts and a lack of economies of scale. However, the dynamic nature of product differentiation fosters innovation and can drive market improvements over time.

Oligopoly

An oligopoly comprises a small number of firms whose market actions are interdependent. This interconnectedness means that the actions of one firm can significantly impact others, often leading to strategic behaviors such as collusion or price-fixing. Oligopolies can wield considerable market power, potentially leading to higher prices and reduced efficiency. On the other hand, economies of scale and the potential for significant research and development investments can bolster innovation and market advancements. Techniques such as game theory are often employed to understand and predict oligopolistic behaviors and outcomes.

Monopoly

A monopoly exists when a single firm dominates the entire market for a particular product or service. Monopolies have substantial market power, allowing them to set prices without competition constraints. This lack of competition can lead to inefficiencies, such as reduced innovation and lower-quality products, alongside higher prices for consumers. Some monopolies are naturally occurring due to high barriers to entry and economies of scale, but regulatory bodies often intervene to mitigate their negative impacts. Price regulation and anti-trust laws are common measures to prevent monopolistic abuses and to enhance market efficiency.

Each of these market structures impacts efficiency differently. Market efficiency is optimal when resources are allocated in a way that maximizes the total benefit to society. In perfectly competitive markets, efficiency is achieved naturally due to the forces of supply and demand. However, in monopolistic competition, oligopoly, and monopoly, market power and strategic behavior can distort supply and demand dynamics, leading to potential inefficiencies.

To assess the efficiency of different market structures, economists use various methods and metrics. Allocative efficiency, productive efficiency, and dynamic efficiency are often evaluated. Allocative efficiency occurs when resources are distributed according to consumer preferences, whereas productive efficiency involves producing goods at the lowest possible cost. Dynamic efficiency looks at how resources are allocated over time, encouraging innovation and improvement.

In real-world scenarios, markets often exhibit characteristics of multiple structures simultaneously, making it imperative to understand the nuances of each. By recognizing the inherent inefficiencies and strengths of each market structure, policymakers and market participants can devise strategies to enhance overall market performance. For example, promoting competition, preventing monopolistic practices, and ensuring transparency can improve market outcomes and drive efficiency.

In conclusion, the efficiency of market structures varies significantly with the nature of competition and the strategic behaviors of firms involved. By examining these structures closely, stakeholders can work towards more efficient market designs that better serve the interests of both consumers and producers.

9.3 Role of Auctions in Market Design

In the intricate landscape of market design, auctions serve as pivotal mechanisms that drive market efficiency and transparency. By understanding the fundamental principles and variations of auctions, investors and traders can better navigate and leverage these frameworks to optimize their market participation.

Auctions act as structured procedures for determining the prices and allocation of assets based on the bids submitted by participants. They play an essential role in establishing fair market values, reducing information asymmetry, and ensuring liquidity. To appreciate the full impact of auctions on market design, we will delve into their primary types, underlying mechanics, and the strategic advantages they offer.

Types of Auctions:

Several auction formats are employed in financial markets, each with distinct characteristics that influence market outcomes:

- **English Auction:** Also known as an ascending price auction, this format involves bidders openly placing progressively higher bids until no higher bids are forthcoming. The highest bidder wins the asset at their bid price. English auctions are commonly used for tangible assets like art and real estate. Their transparency in bid progression helps reveal bidders' valuations, contributing to price discovery.

- **Dutch Auction:** In this descending price format, the auctioneer starts with a high asking price, which is gradually lowered until a participant accepts the price. Dutch auctions are often utilized in the sale of treasury bills and IPOs (Initial Public Offerings). This format can expedite transactions and minimize the risk of collusion among bidders.

- **First-Price Sealed-Bid Auction:** Here, participants submit one confidential bid without knowledge of others' bids, and the highest bidder wins, paying their bid price. This format induces strategic bidding, as participants must carefully balance their bid amounts to win while avoiding overpayment.

- **Second-Price Sealed-Bid Auction (Vickrey Auction):** Similar to the first-price sealed-bid auction, the key difference is that the highest bidder wins but pays the second-highest bid instead. This encourages truthful bidding since paying less than the bid amount mitigates the winner's curse.

Each auction type's unique structure and rules impact how participants strategize their bids, ultimately affecting market transparency and price efficiency.

Mechanics and Strategic Implications:

The mechanics of auctions involve pre-defined rules for bid submission, evaluation, and winner determination. These rules shape participants' behavior and market outcomes. Key components of auction mechanics include:

- **Bid Submission:** The manner in which bids are submitted (open or sealed) significantly influences strategic decision-making. Open bidding allows participants to adjust their strategies based on observed bids, while sealed bidding requires more conjecture and judgment.

- **Pricing Rule:** The pricing rule (first price, second price, etc.) affects participants' willingness to bid their true valuations. Particularly, the second-price rule incentivizes bidders to reveal their true value, enhancing efficiency.

- **Allocation Rule:** This rule defines how the asset is allocated among bidders. In simple auctions, the highest bid wins, but more complex allocation rules can apply in combinatorial auctions where multiple assets are involved.

Strategically, participants must consider their own valuation, the perceived valuations of others, and the auction's rules. For instance, in a first-price sealed-bid auction, bidders may shade their bids below their true valuation to avoid overpayment—a strategy that can lead to lower final prices compared to second-price auctions where bidders bid their true valuations.

Advantages of Auctions in Market Design:

Auctions confer several strategic advantages that promote market efficiency and fairness:

- **Price Discovery:** By aggregating information from multiple participants, auctions aid in discovering an asset's fair market value. This is particularly valuable in markets with limited historical pricing data.

- **Transparency and Fairness:** Auction rules are typically transparent and predetermined, reducing the scope for manipulation and ensuring a level playing field for all participants. This builds market confidence and encourages broader participation.

- **Efficient Allocation:** Auctions often lead to allocative efficiency, where assets are assigned to those who value them most highly. This efficient matching of buyers and sellers enhances overall market liquidity.

- **Reduced Information Asymmetry:** Auctions mitigate the asymmetry of information by compelling participants to reveal their valuations through bids. This reduces the informational advantage of any single participant, fostering a more balanced market environment.

The role of auctions extends beyond mere price setting; they are instrumental in shaping the dynamics of trading and asset allocation, influencing participants' strategies and market behavior. By incorporating well-designed auction mechanisms, markets can enhance their function, efficiency, and participant satisfaction.

Understanding the subtleties and strategic elements of different auction formats enables investors to better anticipate market movements and adapt their approaches, whether participating directly in auctions or interpreting auction-driven market signals. This knowledge empowers market participants to engage more effectively and equitably, fostering a healthier and more resilient trading ecosystem.

9.4 Continuous vs. Discrete Markets

Understanding the distinction between continuous and discrete markets is essential for grasping how different trading environments affect market efficiency, liquidity, and participant behavior. This section delves into the definitions, mechanics, advantages, and limitations of both continuous and discrete markets, providing a comprehensive overview that builds on your foundational knowledge of market design principles.

At its core, a continuous market is one where trading can occur at any moment the market is open. Here, buy and sell orders are matched in real-time, allowing for perpetual price discovery throughout the trading day. Conversely, discrete markets operate using specific time intervals or sessions during which orders are accumulated and matched, often leading to price determination at set points in time.

To better understand these two market types, let's explore their attributes in detail.

Continuous Markets:

In a continuous market, the trading process is dynamic and ongoing. Orders are typically matched using an electronic order book where bids and asks interact in real-time.

The primary advantages include:

- **Enhanced Liquidity:** The constant nature of order matching contributes to higher liquidity, especially in high-volume securities.

- **Timely Price Discovery:** Prices reflect new information almost instantaneously, allowing for more accurate and timely reflections of market sentiment.

- **Flexibility for Traders:** Investors can choose optimal trading times based on their strategies and risk appetites.

Consider the mathematical formulation of a continuous market's order matching process. Assume that orders arrive according to a Poisson process with rate λ. Let $p(t)$ be the price at time t, determined by the intersection of supply and demand functions, $S(p)$ and $D(p)$, respectively. The equilibrium price p^* at any time t can be expressed as:

$$S(p^*(t)) = D(p^*(t))$$

where the functions $S(p)$ and $D(p)$ continuously adjust based on incoming orders.

While continuous markets offer significant benefits, they are not without downsides. The continuous trading environment can exacerbate volatility and lead to higher susceptibility to rapid price swings, particularly in response to market news or events.

Discrete Markets:

Discrete markets, on the other hand, aggregate orders over specified intervals, such as every minute, hour, or even longer sessions like the close of the trading day. At the end of each interval, aggregated orders are matched, and a single clearing price is determined.

The benefits of discrete markets include:

- **Reduced Volatility:** By batching orders, discrete markets can dampen the effects of short-term volatility and provide a more stable trading environment.

- **Improved Transparency:** The periodic matching can offer clearer insights into supply and demand dynamics at specific points in time.

- **Simplicity in Execution:** Execution mechanisms in discrete markets tend to be straightforward, often resulting in fewer strategic complexities for traders.

Consider a discrete-time market where orders are batched and matched every τ units of time. Let $Q_{buy}(t)$ and $Q_{sell}(t)$ represent the total buy and sell quantities at the end of each interval t. The clearing price P_c at the end of interval t is set where the cumulative buy and sell quantities are equal:

$$Q_{buy}(t) = Q_{sell}(t)$$

This batching process can be modeled as:

$$P_c(t) = \frac{1}{2}\left(P_{buy}(t) + P_{sell}(t)\right)$$

where $P_{buy}(t)$ and $P_{sell}(t)$ are the respective prices at which the total buy and sell volumes match.

Despite their stability, discrete markets can introduce inefficiencies such as:

- **Delayed Price Discovery:** Information asymmetries can arise as prices are updated only at discrete intervals, potentially leading to temporary mispricings.

- **Potential for Order Imbalance:** During periods of significant market movement, the time lag in order matching can cause crucial imbalances, impacting liquidity and execution quality.

To contextualize these concepts, consider the equity markets. The Nasdaq operates as a continuous market, matching buy and sell orders throughout the trading day. In contrast, some foreign exchange markets utilize discrete auction mechanisms for certain parities, where order aggregation occurs at predefined times.

To navigate these environments effectively, traders must adapt their strategies. High-frequency traders, for instance, may thrive in continuous markets by leveraging algorithms that capitalize on rapid price changes. Conversely, fundamental investors might find discrete markets more accommodating, as the reduced volatility aligns with longer-term investment horizons.

Ultimately, the choice between continuous and discrete markets hinges on specific trading goals, risk tolerance, and market conditions. A robust understanding of these mechanisms aids in developing tailored strategies that align with the unique characteristics of each market type, fostering informed and strategic trading decisions.

9.5 Measuring Market Efficiency

Market efficiency is a critical concept in trading and investing, as it reflects the degree to which market prices fully incorporate all available information. Efficient markets allow for the accurate valuation of assets, which in turn facilitates better decision-making by investors. Understanding and measuring market efficiency involves several key methodologies and metrics, each providing insights into different facets of market behavior.

To systematically approach the measurement of market efficiency, we start by exploring the Efficient Market Hypothesis (EMH), proposed by Eugene Fama in the 1970s. The EMH posits that in an efficient market, asset prices reflect all available information at any point in time, making it impossible to consistently achieve higher-than-average returns through market timing or stock selection. This hypothesis is foundational to understanding market efficiency and can be empirically tested through various methods.

One prominent way to test for market efficiency is by examining the **random walk theory**, which asserts that price changes are random and unpredictable, implying an efficient market. Empirical tests often involve statistical methods such as the autocorrelation of returns or the variance ratio test to ascertain whether past price movements predict future price changes.

$$Autocorrelation \, of \, Returns \, (\rho_k) = \frac{Cov(r_t, \, r_{t+k})}{Var(r_t)}$$

Here, ρ_k measures the correlation between returns separated by k periods. If ρ_k is significantly different from zero, it suggests predictability, contradicting the random walk theory and hence, market efficiency.

Another technique involves **event studies**, which analyze how quickly and accurately prices respond to new information. This method investigates the abnormal returns around specific events, such as earnings announcements or economic reports. If markets are efficient, any new information should be instantaneously integrated into prices.

$$AR_{it} = R_{it} - E(R_{it})$$

In this equation, AR_{it} represents the abnormal return of security i at time t; R_{it} is the actual return, and $E(R_{it})$ is the expected return. Efficient markets are expected to show no significant abnormal returns after the event, indicating that prices reflect all available information.

Additionally, econometric models can be utilized to measure market efficiency. These models often employ regression analysis to check the relationship between returns and information variables such as earnings, dividends, or macroeconomic indicators. For instance, the regression model for analyzing the informational efficiency of dividends might look like:

$$R_t = \alpha + \beta D_t + \epsilon_t$$

In this model, R_t represents the return at time t, D_t is the dividend, and ϵ_t is the error term. The coefficient β indicates how responsive returns are to changes in dividends.

Furthermore, analyzing **market microstructure** data provides granular insights into efficiency. Metrics such as bid-ask spreads, order book depth, and trade execution quality reflect the informational environment of the market. Narrow bid-ask spreads and deep order books typically signify high efficiency, as they indicate low transaction costs and robust liquidity.

$$Bid - Ask\ Spread = \frac{Ask\ Price - Bid\ Price}{(Ask\ Price + Bid\ Price)/2}$$

High-frequency data analysis leverages advanced algorithmic techniques, capturing the nuanced price dynamics in millisecond intervals, which can be crucial for detecting and understanding market inefficiencies that might not be apparent in lower-frequency data.

Lastly, a practical yet insightful measure of market efficiency is through **portfolio performance analysis**. If markets are efficient, then portfolios managed based on public information should not systematically outperform the market. Performance metrics like the Sharpe Ratio or Jensen's Alpha are used to gauge whether any observed outperformance is due to skill or merely luck.

$$Sharpe\ Ratio = \frac{R_p - R_f}{\sigma_p}$$

$$Jensen's\ Alpha = R_i - [R_f + \beta_i(R_m - R_f)]$$

In these equations, R_p is the portfolio return, R_f the risk-free rate, σ_p the portfolio's standard deviation, R_i the individual security's return, β_i the security's beta, and R_m the market return.

Through these various methodologies, investors and researchers can rigorously assess the efficiency of markets, facilitating better strategic decisions and contributing to a deeper understanding of market dynamics. It is clear that while perfect efficiency is an ideal, real markets exhibit varying degrees of efficiency influenced by factors like information dissemination, transaction costs, and investor behavior. By continually refining these measurement techniques, the quest to understand and enhance market efficiency remains an evolving and engaging endeavor.

9.6 Market Failures and Inefficiencies

Understanding market failures and inefficiencies is crucial for both traders and regulators aiming to optimize market functioning. Market failures occur when there is an inefficient allocation of resources in a market, leading to a loss of economic value. These inefficiencies can arise due to various reasons, including information asymmetries, market power, externalities, and transaction costs. Recognizing these failures helps in designing better regulatory measures and trading strategies to mitigate adverse effects on market efficiency.

One of the most prominent sources of market inefficiency is asymmetric information, where some market participants possess information that others do not. This can lead to adverse selection and moral hazard problems. Adverse selection occurs when traders with better information exploit those with less information, which can result in markets becoming dominated by poor-quality assets. For example, in the stock market, insiders who have non-public information may engage in trades that unfairly benefit them at the expense of uninformed investors, undermining overall market confidence.

Moral hazard, on the other hand, arises when traders take on excessive risks because they do not bear the full consequences of these risks. This is often seen in financial institutions that trade on behalf of clients but might engage in speculative activities that yield high returns along with high risks. The 2008 financial crisis is a prime example, where institutions engaged in risky mortgage-backed securities trading without adequate consideration of potential fallout, leading to widespread economic instability.

Market power is another significant cause of inefficiency. When individual participants or a group of participants can control prices or market supply, they can manipulate the market to their advantage. Monopolistic or oligopolistic scenarios reduce competition and can lead to pricing that does not reflect the true equilibrium of supply and demand. For instance, in certain commodity markets, a few large players might control the majority of supply, allowing them to set prices that maximize their profits, rather than letting the market control prices naturally.

Externalities represent another source of inefficiency. These are costs or benefits that affect third parties who are not directly involved in a transaction. Negative externalities, such as environmental pollution, can lead to overproduction of harmful goods if the market does not internalize these external costs. Conversely, positive externalities, such as technological innovations, might be underproduced if the market fails to adequately reward creators, leading to suboptimal investment in research and development.

Transaction costs, including fees, taxes, and the cost of acquiring information, can also contribute to market inefficiencies. High transaction costs can discourage trading and reduce liquidity, making it more difficult for markets to reach efficient outcomes. For instance, if the costs of trading stocks are too high, investors may be less inclined to participate, leading to lower overall market activity and higher spreads between bid and ask prices.

In addition to these broad categories, specific market imperfections can exacerbate inefficiencies. For example, the phenomenon of trading delays and high-frequency trading can create temporary imbalances and price distortions. Algorithmic trading, while beneficial in terms of liquidity provision, can sometimes lead to flash crashes where automated trading systems malfunction, causing rapid and significant price changes that can erode market confidence.

Effective regulation and strategic market design can mitigate these failures. Regulatory measures such as enforcing transparency, reducing informational asymmetries, and setting limits on market power are essential. Moreover, designing markets that minimize externalities and lower transaction costs can foster more efficient trading environments. Certification systems, better disclosure norms, and innovative trading mechanisms such as frequent batch auctions can also help in reducing market inefficiencies by ensuring that prices more accurately reflect true value.

By comprehensively understanding these varied sources of inefficiencies, market participants can better navigate the complexities of trading environments, while regulators can develop more effective frameworks to enhance overall market efficiency. This multi-faceted approach ensures that markets are not only efficient but also equitable and robust against failures that can undermine economic stability.

9.7 Improving Market Efficiency through Design

Market efficiency is pivotal to the effective functioning of financial markets, ensuring that prices fully reflect available information and resources are optimally allocated. Improving market efficiency through design requires an intricate understanding of market dynamics, participant behavior, and technological advancements. This section delves deeply into various mechanisms and strategies that can be employed to enhance market efficiency, rooted in empirical research and theoretical principles.

One of the primary avenues for improving market efficiency is through the optimization of trading platforms. Digital trading platforms, with their fast execution capabilities and real-time data dissemination, reduce latency and the costs associated with information asymmetry. High-frequency trading (HFT), for instance, capitalizes on these advancements by executing numerous orders at incredibly high speeds, thereby contributing to price discovery and liquidity provision. However, the benefits of HFT must be balanced against potential drawbacks, such as the risk of market manipulation and flash crashes. Effective regulatory oversight becomes crucial here, mandating transparency and implementing safeguards to mitigate undue volatility.

Another crucial design aspect is the structuring of order types and market orders. The inclusion of various order types, such as limit orders and stop-loss orders, allows traders to manage their risks more effectively and contributes to market depth. Enhanced market depth, in turn, tends to reduce bid-ask spreads and improve price continuity. A meticulously designed order matching algorithm can further enhance efficiency by prioritizing orders in a way that reduces slippage and maintains fair access for all participants. For instance, the use of time-weighted average price (TWAP) and volume-weighted average price (VWAP) algorithms can provide more equitable trading conditions and prevent market impact from large orders.

Market efficiency can also be significantly bolstered through the implementation of circuit breakers and volatility controls. These mechanisms help in tempering excessive price movements and providing a cooling-off period during extreme volatility. By temporarily halting trading activities, circuit breakers prevent panic selling and allow traders to reassess market conditions, fostering stability and rational decision-making. The design of such emergency controls should be nuanced, ensuring they are activated under conditions that genuinely warrant them, without unnecessarily obstructing natural market flows.

Increasing overall market transparency is another fundamental strategy for enhancing efficiency. Transparency reduces information asymmetry, ensuring that all market participants have access to the same data at the same time. This can be facilitated through stringent reporting requirements for trades, mandatory disclosures of short positions, and the public availability of order book data. Transparent markets deter manipulative practices and build confidence among investors, thereby promoting a more robust trading environment.

The role of technology in improving market efficiency cannot be overstated. Blockchain, for example, offers a decentralized and immutable ledger for recording transactions, which can enhance post-trade transparency and reduce settlement times. Smart contracts, powered by blockchain, can automate contractual agreements and ensure their execution without the need for intermediaries, lowering transaction costs and enhancing reliability. Additionally, advanced analytical tools and machine learning algorithms provide deeper insights into market behavior, enabling more informed decision-making processes.

Regulatory frameworks play an essential role in market design. Regulators must strike a balance between fostering innovation and maintaining orderly markets. Policies that promote fairness, such as best execution rules, ensure that traders receive the most advantageous terms available. Cross-border collaborations among regulatory authorities can further harmonize regulations, reducing arbitrage opportunities and contributing to global market efficiency.

Adopting a holistic approach to market design by incorporating feedback mechanisms can lead to continuous improvement in market efficiency. Regular analysis of trading patterns, market anomalies, and participant feedback allows for dynamic adaptations to market rules and infrastructure. Real-time monitoring and data analytics facilitate the identification and swift rectification of inefficiencies or potential points of failure within the market system.

Ultimately, the goal of market design should be to create a resilient framework that adapts to evolving market conditions while fostering fairness, transparency, and efficiency. By leveraging cutting-edge technology, innovative trading mechanisms, and robust regulatory oversight, market efficiency can be significantly enhanced, benefitting all participants and contributing to the overall stability of the financial system.

Chapter 10

Information and Asymmetry in Markets

This chapter explores the concept of information asymmetry in financial markets, identifying its various sources and impacts on market behavior. It delves into phenomena such as adverse selection and moral hazard, and discusses mechanisms designed to mitigate these issues. The chapter also examines the implications of insider trading and market abuse, highlighting their effects on market integrity. Finally, it considers the role of information in enhancing market efficiency, emphasizing the critical need for transparency and equitable access to information for all market participants.

10.1 Concept of Information Asymmetry

Understanding the concept of information asymmetry is crucial for grasping the deeper nuances of financial markets. Information asymmetry occurs when one party in a transaction holds more or better information compared to the other party. This imbalance can have significant implications for market behavior, asset pricing, and overall market integrity.

In financial markets, information asymmetry often arises between buyers and sellers. For instance, a company's management typically possesses more detailed and timely knowledge about the firm's perfor-mance, prospects, and risks than outside investors. This uneven distri-bution of information can lead to suboptimal decision-making and mar-ket inefficiencies.

To explore this further, consider a typical stock market transaction. When an investor decides to buy shares of a company, they rely on publicly available information such as financial statements, news re-leases, and market analyses. However, if there exists private informa-tion that is not accessible to the general public, those with access to such data can potentially exploit it to their advantage. This exploita-tion manifests in several ways, such as through insider trading, where individuals trade based on non-public, material information, or in the manipulation of stock prices.

Mathematically, the concept of information asymmetry can be repre-sented through Bayesian models. For instance, let us denote the true value of a security by V, which is recognized by an insider but is only partially known to an outside investor. The investor forms a belief about V based on observable signals S. The investor's estimation can be modeled using a conditional expectation:

$$E(V \mid S) = \int_{-\infty}^{\infty} v f_{V|S}(v|s)\, dv$$

Here, $f_{V|S}(v|s)$ represents the conditional probability density function of V given S. The higher the discrepancy between the insider's knowl-edge and the public signal S, the greater the information asymmetry.

Information asymmetry also plays a critical role in the adverse selection problem. Adverse selection, a term initially coined in the insurance in-dustry, describes a situation where sellers have more information about the quality of a product than buyers. In financial markets, adverse se-lection can make it difficult for investors to distinguish between good and bad investments, thus leading to higher market volatility and less efficient capital allocation.

Moreover, information asymmetry can result in moral hazard, where one party engages in risky behavior because they do not bear the full consequences of that risk. For example, a company with inside knowl-edge about impending financial difficulties might engage in aggressive borrowing and investment strategies, transferring the risk to uninformed investors.

Numerous theoretical frameworks and models have been developed to address and analyze the effects of information asymmetry. A corner-stone of these is Akerlof's 'Market for Lemons' model, which illustrates how information asymmetry in the used car market leads to an overall decline in the quality of goods traded. Translating this into financial markets, poor-quality investments drive out high-quality investments, leading to a market filled with undervalued or overvalued securities.

It is essential to recognize that while information asymmetry can lead to negative outcomes, certain regulatory mechanisms and market practices aim to mitigate its impact. These include stringent disclosure requirements, insider trading regulations, and the promotion of market transparency. Additionally, technological advancements, such as the use of blockchain for ensuring real-time information dissemination, are progressively enhancing the flow of information in markets.

In conclusion, the concept of information asymmetry is pivotal to understanding market dynamics. It underscores the importance of information distribution in achieving market efficiency and upholding market integrity. The subsequent sections will delve deeper into the various sources and impacts of information asymmetry, and the mechanisms designed to counteract these imbalances in the financial markets.

10.2   Sources of Information Asymmetry

Information asymmetry in financial markets arises when one party in a transaction possesses more or superior information compared to the other. This imbalance can lead to inefficiencies and injustices, affecting both market behavior and individual investment decisions. Understanding the sources of information asymmetry is crucial for identifying potential risks and developing strategies to mitigate them. This section delves into the various origins of information asymmetry, offering insights into how they manifest and impact financial markets.

One primary source of information asymmetry is the heterogeneous access to corporate information. Firms disclose information through various channels, including financial statements, press releases, and mandatory filings. However, these disclosures are often not distributed uniformly to all market participants. Insiders, such as executives and board members, typically have access to material non-public information about the company's financial health, strategic plans, and potential risks before the general public. This access allows them to make informed trading decisions that can disadvantage other investors who rely solely on public disclosures.

Another significant source is the complexity of financial products and markets. Financial instruments, such as derivatives, structured products, and even some conventional securities, can be complex and difficult for average investors to understand fully. Financial institutions and sophisticated investors, equipped with advanced knowledge and analytical tools, can exploit this complexity. For example, the 2008 financial crisis highlighted how intricate mortgage-backed securities and credit default swaps created severe information asymmetry between financial institutions and the broader market, leading to substantial losses for less-informed investors.

Technological advancements have also contributed to information asymmetry, particularly through algorithmic and high-frequency trading (HFT). These trading strategies involve the use of sophisticated algorithms to execute orders at speeds and frequencies unattainable by human traders. Firms specializing in HFT often gain access to electronic order books, market microstructure data, and other granular datasets that provide them with a superior vantage point. This allows them to anticipate market movements and execute trades milliseconds before others, creating a distinct information advantage.

Moreover, research and analytical capabilities represent another crucial source. Large institutional investors and hedge funds typically have extensive research departments staffed with analysts and financial experts who scrutinize market data, corporate filings, and economic indicators to generate proprietary insights. In contrast, retail investors and smaller firms may lack the resources to conduct such in-depth analyses, thus operating at an informational disadvantage.

Public information leakage is also a common source of information asymmetry. Sensitive information can gradually leak into the market before an official announcement, often reaching certain investors ahead of others. This can occur through informal channels, such as industry networks, or more dubious means, including whisper campaigns and insider tips. Consequently, those privy to early information can trade on it, reaping benefits long before the broader market has a chance to react.

Regulatory environments also play a vital role in either mitigating or exacerbating information asymmetry. Markets with stringent disclosure requirements, robust enforcement of insider trading laws, and transparent reporting standards tend to exhibit lower levels of information asymmetry. Conversely, markets with lax regulations or inconsistent enforcement create opportunities for information arbitrage, where better-informed traders exploit less-informed counterparts.

Lastly, psychological and behavioral differences among market participants can lead to information asymmetry. Behavioral finance studies indicate that cognitive biases, such as overconfidence or fear of missing out (FOMO), can cause investors to misinterpret or underutilize available information. Experienced traders or firms with behavioral insights can predict and capitalize on these biases, generating profits at the expense of less rational market participants.

Understanding these sources is fundamental for navigating and potentially rectifying the imbalances they create. By recognizing how information asymmetry arises from corporate disclosures, product complexity, technological advancements, research capabilities, information leakage, regulatory frameworks, and behavioral biases, investors can better evaluate risks and make more informed decisions in financial markets. As we move forward, it becomes imperative to devise and implement strategies that can bridge these information gaps, fostering a more equitable and efficient market environment for all participants.

10.3 Impact of Asymmetric Information on Markets

The impact of asymmetric information on financial markets is profound, shaping behavior and outcomes in ways that can significantly influence market dynamics, pricing, and participation. When one party in a transaction possesses more or better information than the other, it creates an imbalance that can lead to inefficiencies and distortions. Understanding these impacts is crucial to comprehending the broader mechanics of market microstructure.

The presence of asymmetric information can give rise to several notable phenomena within the financial markets:

One of the primary effects is *adverse selection*, where markets may fail to allocate resources efficiently due to the information gap between buyers and sellers. For example, in the context of the stock market, if insiders or more informed traders possess private information about a company's true value, they might only trade when they have a favorable position, leaving less informed traders at a disadvantage. This can lead to a situation where the market undervalues or overvalues securities,

163

distorting the overall price formation process.

To mathematically illustrate adverse selection, consider the market pricing model where the true value of a stock is represented as V. Informed traders know V precisely, while uninformed traders estimate V based on available public information, yielding an expected value $E[V]$. If ΔV represents the information advantage of the informed traders, the transaction price P might deviate from $E[V]$, causing potential mispricing:

$$P = E[V] \pm \Delta V.$$

Here, the term ΔV encapsulates the degree of adverse selection impacting the transaction.

Another significant consequence is *moral hazard*, where the behavior of one party changes to the detriment of another after a transaction has occurred, often because the less informed party cannot fully monitor the actions of the better-informed party. In investing, moral hazard may manifest when fund managers, given control over substantial assets, might take higher risks, knowing that the negative repercussions of their actions would predominantly affect the investors rather than themselves.

The presence of asymmetric information also affects market participation and liquidity. Less informed traders may become hesitant to engage in markets where they perceive a severe informational disadvantage, fearing exploitation by better-informed traders. This reluctance can reduce market liquidity, increase bid-ask spreads, and enhance trading costs, resulting in a less efficient market environment.

The broader market structure can also be impacted. In markets where asymmetric information is prevalent, market makers may adjust their strategies to protect themselves from potential losses incurred by trading with more informed participants. They might widen bid-ask spreads to compensate for information risk, reflected by the adverse selection component in the bid-ask spread formulation:

$$\text{Spread} = \text{Order Processing Cost} + \text{Adverse Selection Cost.}$$

Here, the *Adverse Selection Cost* is directly tied to the degree of information asymmetry, incentivizing liquidity providers to adjust spreads accordingly.

Furthermore, this information imbalance can exacerbate *price volatility*. Informed traders acting on private information can generate sharp and rapid price movements, especially if they trade in large volumes. Markets may experience increased volatility as prices adjust quickly to new information that is unevenly distributed among participants. This phenomenon often results in a more turbulent trading environment, discouraging long-term investment and fostering a speculative atmosphere.

The complex interplay between informed and uninformed traders can create a feedback loop, potentially leading to what is known as *cascade effects*. In such scenarios, uninformed traders, observing the actions of informed traders, may attempt to infer information from their trades and adjust their strategies accordingly. If a significant volume of trading occurs based on inferred information, it can amplify the initial price movement, further driving prices away from fundamental values.

In more extreme cases, information asymmetry can lead to *market breakdowns*. If the informational gap between participants becomes too wide, trust in the market's price discovery mechanism diminishes. For instance, in markets for thinly traded or opaque securities, where information asymmetry is typically more pronounced, liquidity can dry up entirely, leading to market failure. Investors may withhold trading altogether, opting to exit the market rather than face untenable risks.

The consequences of asymmetric information underscore the importance of transparency and equitable information dissemination. Measures aimed at improving transparency—such as strict disclosure requirements, enhanced regulatory oversight, and the promotion of fair trading practices—are essential tools in mitigating the adverse impacts of information imbalances. Efforts to facilitate better access to information for all market participants help in leveling the playing field, thereby fostering a more efficient and resilient market structure.

By understanding the impact that asymmetric information can have on markets, investors and regulators can better appreciate the need for robust informational frameworks and the role they play in promoting market integrity and stability. Thus, addressing and managing asymmetric information remains a fundamental objective in the pursuit of well-functioning financial markets.

10.4 Adverse Selection and Moral Hazard

Adverse selection and moral hazard are two critical concepts stemming from the broader theme of information asymmetry in financial markets. Understanding these phenomena is essential for investors, traders, and financial institutions as they navigate the complexities of market interactions. Both adverse selection and moral hazard can significantly impact market dynamics, trading strategies, and overall market efficiency.

Adverse selection arises when one party in a transaction possesses information that the other party does not, leading to suboptimal decision-making. In the context of financial markets, adverse selection typically occurs when sellers have more information about the quality or risk profile of an asset than buyers. This imbalance can result in the market being dominated by low-quality or high-risk assets, as informed sellers are more inclined to offload inferior assets to uninformed buyers.

To illustrate this concept, consider the market for corporate bonds. Suppose there is a pool of bonds with varying credit qualities, ranging from high-grade (low risk) to junk bonds (high risk). If investors cannot readily distinguish between the high-quality and lower-quality bonds due to insufficient information, they are likely to offer prices that reflect an average risk level. Consequently, issuers of high-grade bonds might withdraw from the market, unwilling to accept prices that undervalue their bonds. This scenario leaves more junk bonds relative to high-grade bonds in the market, which further exacerbates the problem. Economists George Akerlof described this dynamic as "The Market for Lemons," where the quality of goods traded in a market can degrade in the presence of information asymmetry.

Mathematically, we can model adverse selection using probability and expected values. Let P_i denote the price of a bond, where $i \in \{high, low\}$. Assuming the probabilities of encountering high-quality and low-quality bonds in a mixed market are p_h and p_l, respectively, the expected price $E(P)$ from the buyer's perspective is:

$$E(P) = p_h \cdot P_{\text{high}} + p_l \cdot P_{\text{low}}$$

If $P_{\text{high}} > E(P)$ and $P_{\text{low}} < E(P)$, sellers of high-quality bonds (high P_i) will likely exit the market, leaving predominantly low-quality bonds. This adverse selection drives market efficiency down and increases the risk of transactions.

Moral hazard, on the other hand, occurs when one party in a transaction can take on risks because they do not bear the full consequences of their actions, knowing that the other party will incur the costs. In financial markets, moral hazard often surfaces after a transaction has been completed. For instance, in the relationship between a borrower and a lender, if the lender cannot perfectly monitor the borrower's actions, the borrower might engage in riskier behavior after obtaining a loan, since the downside risk is shared or primarily borne by the lender.

A significant manifestation of moral hazard can be observed in the banking sector. Consider the case of banks that engage in high-risk trading strategies. If these banks are perceived as "too big to fail," they might be emboldened to take excessive risks, assuming they will receive government bailouts in the event of failure. This behavior, exacerbated by the asymmetry in risk-sharing, can lead to systemic risks, as evidenced by the 2008 financial crisis.

To mitigate adverse selection and moral hazard, various mechanisms have been devised. For adverse selection, information disclosure rules and due diligence procedures are implemented to reduce information gaps. For instance, financial regulations mandating detailed prospectuses and regular financial disclosures enable investors to make more informed decisions, reducing the likelihood of adverse selection.

Addressing moral hazard involves aligning incentives more closely between parties. Performance-based compensation, covenants, and monitoring mechanisms help ensure that actions taken by one party do not disproportionately expose the other party to undue risk. In the lending example, lenders might require regular financial reporting from borrowers or include restrictive covenants in loan agreements to limit risk-taking behaviors.

Understanding and mitigating adverse selection and moral hazard is vital for maintaining market integrity and efficiency. By addressing these issues through regulatory frameworks and prudent practices, markets can function more effectively, sustaining investor confidence and fostering a more stable financial system.

10.5 Mechanisms to Mitigate Information Asymmetry

In financial markets, information asymmetry occurs when one party possesses more or better information than the other, often leading to an imbalance that can result in inefficiencies and potential abuses. To counteract the detrimental effects of information asymmetry, several mechanisms have been developed and implemented. These mechanisms strive to level the playing field, ensuring that all market participants have fair access to the information they need to make informed decisions. This section will explore various strategies and tools that help mitigate information asymmetry, enhancing market transparency and integrity.

One primary mechanism for reducing information asymmetry is the establishment of stringent disclosure requirements. Regulatory bodies such as the Securities and Exchange Commission (SEC) in the United States mandate that public companies provide comprehensive and timely disclosures of critical financial and operational information. By enforcing rigorous reporting standards, these regulations ensure that both investors and analysts have access to consistent, reliable data, which is crucial for making informed investment decisions. These disclosures typically include quarterly and annual financial statements, executive compensation details, and any material changes in the company's operations or financial condition.

Another significant measure is the implementation of fair access to information through equal dissemination. This principle stipulates that all market-relevant information should be disseminated to all market participants simultaneously. For instance, when a company releases its earnings report, it must ensure that the report is available to all investors at the same time through widely accessible channels such as press releases and official filings on regulatory websites. The advent of electronic communication networks (ECNs) and advanced information technology has facilitated the equitable distribution of information, minimizing opportunities for certain traders to gain an unfair advantage.

Market makers and exchanges also play a pivotal role in mitigating information asymmetry. Through the provision of liquidity and continuous pricing, market makers help to ensure that trading can occur even in the presence of uncertain information. They absorb order imbalances and reduce volatility, which can be exacerbated by asymmetric information. Moreover, modern exchanges often employ sophisticated surveillance systems to monitor trading activity, detect unusual patterns, and identify potential cases of market abuse. These surveillance systems are critical in maintaining fair and orderly markets, as they can quickly address and rectify any discrepancies that arise due to information asymmetry.

Insider trading regulations are another key component in the fight against information asymmetry. Laws and regulations expressly prohibit trading on material non-public information. Regulatory bodies enforce these rules through a combination of monitoring, investigation, and prosecution of violators. By deterring insider trading, these regulations help to protect the integrity of the market, ensuring that no investor is disadvantaged because others have access to privileged information. High-profile prosecutions and significant penalties serve as strong deterrents against such unethical behavior.

The role of financial analysts and rating agencies cannot be overstated in enhancing information symmetry. Analysts scrutinize companies and industries, producing research reports that provide valuable insights and forecasts. These reports are disseminated widely, enabling investors to make more informed decisions. Rating agencies, meanwhile, provide independent assessments of the creditworthiness of companies and financial products, promoting greater transparency in credit markets. However, it is important to ensure that these entities operate without conflicts of interest that could compromise the impartiality of their analysis and ratings.

Advancements in technology, particularly the rise of algorithmic trading and artificial intelligence, have also contributed to the mitigation of information asymmetry. Algorithms can process vast amounts of data at incredible speeds, identifying trends and patterns that might not be visible to human traders. By leveraging big data and machine learning, these systems can provide real-time analysis and insights, enabling a more informed and reactive trading environment. Furthermore, technology-driven platforms and fintech innovations have democratized access to financial information, allowing retail investors to access tools and resources that were once reserved for institutional players.

Finally, market education and literacy programs play a crucial role in addressing information asymmetry. By equipping investors with the knowledge and skills to understand and interpret financial information, these programs help to create a more informed and competent investor base. Educational initiatives can take many forms, from public seminars and workshops to online courses and certification programs. A well-educated investor is better positioned to evaluate information critically and make sound investment decisions.

Through these various mechanisms, the financial markets strive to mitigate the impact of information asymmetry, fostering a more transparent, efficient, and equitable trading environment. By continually evolving and adapting these measures, regulators, market participants, and technology providers work together to uphold the integrity and stability of the markets, ensuring that all participants can engage on a level playing field.

10.6   Insider Trading and Market Abuse

The phenomenon of insider trading and market abuse is pivotal in understanding the integrity and functioning of financial markets. At its core, insider trading involves the buying or selling of a security by someone who has access to material, non-public information about the security. Market abuse encompasses a broader range of unethical and illegal activities that create unfair advantages in the marketplace. Together, these practices undermine the principles of fairness, transparency, and equal opportunity that are essential for the efficient operation of financial markets.

Insider trading is often considered a direct consequence of information asymmetry. When certain individuals or entities have access to exclusive information, they can exploit it to gain unfair trading advantages. This practice is not only ethically questionable but also illegal in most jurisdictions. Institutions such as the Securities and Exchange Commission (SEC) in the United States have stringent regulations to combat insider trading and protect the interests of all investors.

To grasp the mechanics of insider trading, it is essential to understand the types of information classified as material and non-public. Material information refers to any data that a reasonable investor would consider important in making an investment decision. Examples include financial results, corporate mergers or acquisitions, product launches, and significant litigation matters. Non-public information, as the term suggests, is information not yet disclosed to the general public.

> "Material, non-public information creates an uneven playing field, allowing insiders to profit at the expense of regular investors." — Financial Expert

Consider the case of a corporate executive who learns about an upcoming merger that will significantly increase the company's stock value. If the executive purchases shares before the merger is public knowledge, they gain an unfair advantage over other investors. When such activities are discovered, enforcement agencies impose severe penalties, including fines and imprisonment.

Market abuse extends beyond insider trading, incorporating a variety of illicit activities aimed at manipulating market prices and trading volumes. Market manipulation can take several forms, such as:

- **Pump and Dump**: Promoters artificially inflate the price of a stock through false or misleading statements. Once the price is elevated, they sell their shares at the inflated price, leading to sharp declines and substantial losses for other investors.

- **Spoofing**: Traders place large orders to give the illusion of demand or supply, then cancel them before execution. This creates a misleading impression about the market conditions, influencing prices.

- **Front Running**: This occurs when a broker executes orders on a security for its own account while taking advantage of advance knowledge of pending orders from clients.

These practices distort market prices and erode investor confidence. Regulators employ various strategies to detect and prevent market abuse. Advanced surveillance systems monitor trading patterns for irregularities, while whistleblower programs incentivize reporting of suspicious activities.

The legal framework surrounding insider trading and market abuse is complex and evolves continuously to address new tactics employed by market offenders. Legal provisions such as Rule 10b-5 under the Securities Exchange Act of 1934 prohibit any act or omission resulting in fraud or deceit in connection with the purchase or sale of any security. Regulatory bodies frequently update compliance requirements to incorporate technological advancements and close loopholes that could be exploited.

A critical aspect of combating insider trading and market abuse is enhancing market transparency. Companies are required to disclose material information promptly to ensure that all investors have equal access to vital data. Additionally, the implementation of strict corporate governance practices helps mitigate misuse of insider information.

Educating market participants about the legal and ethical ramifications of insider trading and market abuse also plays a significant role. Corporate training programs and investor education initiatives create awareness and promote ethical behavior among all stakeholders.

Ultimately, tackling insider trading and market abuse is fundamental to maintaining market integrity and efficiency. Ensuring that markets operate on a level playing field fosters investor confidence and encourages broader participation, which are crucial for the healthy functioning of financial systems worldwide. By systematically addressing these issues through stringent regulation, surveillance, and education, markets can strive towards fairness and transparency, aligning closely with the principles of equitable access to information for all participants.

10.7   Role of Information in Market Efficiency

Information plays an essential role in the efficient functioning of financial markets. Market efficiency refers to the degree to which market prices fully reflect all available information. In an efficient market, securities are priced accurately, thus making it impossible for investors to consistently achieve excess returns through exploiting informational advantages. To understand the role of information in market efficiency, we must explore various facets, including the Efficient Market Hypothesis (EMH), information dissemination methods, and the impact of technology on information flow.

Efficient Market Hypothesis (EMH): The EMH, formulated by Eugene Fama in the 1970s, posits that financial markets are "efficient" in processing information. It suggests three forms of market efficiency:

- *Weak-form efficiency*: In this form, current stock prices reflect all historical price data. Hence, technical analysis, which relies on past price movements, cannot consistently yield excess returns.

- *Semi-strong-form efficiency*: Here, prices reflect all publicly available information, including financial statements, news releases, and economic reports. Thus, fundamental analysis becomes ineffective in predicting future price movements and obtaining superior returns.

- *Strong-form efficiency*: This form asserts that prices incorporate all information, both public and private (insider information), making it impossible for any investor to achieve abnormal profits.

Information Dissemination: Efficient markets depend on the rapid and widespread dissemination of information to all market participants. Various channels ensure information flow, including financial news media, corporate disclosures, analyst reports, and regulatory filings. The advent of digital platforms and social media has further accelerated information dissemination, reducing time lags and increasing market responsiveness.

Technological Advancements: The rise of algorithmic trading, big data analytics, and artificial intelligence has revolutionized the way information is processed and used in financial markets. Algorithms can analyze vast datasets in real-time, identifying patterns and trends that human traders might overlook. This technological edge contributes to market efficiency by:

- Enhancing liquidity: Algorithmic trading strategies like market making ensure continuous buying and selling, narrowing bid-ask spreads and improving price discovery.

- Reducing latency: High-frequency trading (HFT) leverages advanced algorithms and low-latency networks to execute trades in microseconds, ensuring prices quickly reflect new information.

- Minimizing errors: Automated systems reduce the likelihood of human errors, maintaining the integrity and consistency of market operations.

Transparency and Regulatory Oversight: Transparency is a cornerstone of market efficiency. Regulatory bodies, such as the Securities and Exchange Commission (SEC) in the United States, enforce rules mandating timely and accurate disclosure of material information by publicly traded companies. Initiatives like Regulation Fair Disclosure (Reg FD) aim to curb informational disparities, ensuring that all investors have equal access to significant corporate data.

While complete market efficiency is an ideal state, real-world markets often exhibit varying degrees of inefficiency. Factors such as information asymmetry, behavioral biases, and transaction costs can lead to temporary mispricings. However, the mechanisms of arbitrage—as informed traders exploit price discrepancies—tend to restore equilibrium, reinforcing the efficiency paradigm.

Information's role in market efficiency underscores the importance of fostering an environment where information is readily available, accurate, and disseminated equitably. Informed investors make better decisions, contributing to a virtuous cycle that enhances the robustness and reliability of financial markets. This interplay between information and market efficiency not only promotes fair pricing but also engenders trust and confidence among market participants, ensuring the long-term viability and growth of the financial system.

Chapter 11

Risk Management in Quantitative Trading

This chapter focuses on the fundamentals of risk management in quantitative trading, discussing the various types of risks traders face. It covers statistical measures of risk and explores different risk management strategies and tools. Topics include portfolio diversification, stress testing, and scenario analysis. The chapter also addresses regulatory requirements pertinent to risk management, emphasizing their importance in maintaining financial stability and mitigating potential losses.

11.1   Fundamentals of Risk Management

To thrive in quantitative trading, one must first master the fundamentals of risk management. Managing risk is essential to preserving capital, achieving stable returns, and preventing catastrophic losses that can derail not only individual portfolios but entire financial systems. This foundational section sets the stage for understanding risk management by exploring core principles and practices that are indispensable for any trader.

Risk management in trading is the process of identifying, analyzing, and mitigating uncertainties that can negatively impact investment performance. At its core, it revolves around the quantification of potential losses and the implementation of strategies to control or eliminate such risks. Below, we will delve deeper into several key aspects that form the bedrock of effective risk management.

1. Identifying Risks

The first step in risk management is the identification of risks. Traders face various types of risks, including market risk, credit risk, liquidity risk, operational risk, and systemic risk. Each of these risks can arise from different sources and can have unique impacts on a trading strategy.

Market Risk refers to the possibility of an investor experiencing losses due to factors that affect the overall performance of financial markets. These can include changes in interest rates, foreign exchange rates, and commodity prices.

Credit Risk involves the potential for a loss resulting from a borrower's failure to repay a loan or meet contractual obligations. This risk is particularly pertinent for fixed income securities and is a critical consideration for credit traders.

Liquidity Risk arises when an investor is unable to buy or sell an asset without causing a significant impact on its price. This can be a major issue in asset classes that do not trade frequently.

Operational Risk stems from failures in internal processes, systems, or people, and can include risks such as fraud, legal issues, or technology failures.

Systemic Risk is the danger that the failure of one entity within the financial system will cause a chain reaction, leading to the collapse of various interconnected institutions.

2. Quantifying Risk

Once risks are identified, the next step is to quantify them. This involves determining the potential impact of each risk and the probability of its occurrence. Quantitative tools and techniques, such as Value at Risk (VaR), Conditional Value at Risk (CVaR), and stress testing, are employed to measure and assess risks.

The *Value at Risk (VaR)* is a widely used risk measure that estimates the potential loss in value of a portfolio over a defined period for a given confidence interval. Formally, it is defined as:

$$VaR_\alpha(X) = -\inf\{x \in \mathbb{R} : P(X \leq x) > \alpha\} \tag{11.1}$$

where α is the confidence level (e.g., 95% or 99

Conditional Value at Risk (CVaR), also known as Expected Shortfall, provides an estimate of the expected loss exceeding the VaR threshold. It is defined as the conditional expectation of losses given that they are beyond the VaR level:

$$CVaR_\alpha(X) = E\left[X \mid X \geq VaR_\alpha(X)\right] \tag{11.2}$$

3. Mitigating Risk

With risks identified and quantified, the next task is to mitigate them—implementing strategies to reduce the potential impact of these risks. Common risk mitigation techniques include diversification, hedging, and the use of stop-loss orders.

Diversification involves spreading investments across various asset classes, sectors, or geographies to reduce the overall risk. The rationale is that a well-diversified portfolio is less likely to be significantly impacted by a single adverse event.

Hedging is a strategy used to offset potential losses in one investment by making another. For example, a trader might use financial derivatives, such as options or futures, to hedge against the risk of adverse price movements.

Stop-loss orders are used to automatically sell a security when it reaches a certain price, thereby limiting potential losses. This is a particularly useful tool for managing market risk in volatile trading environments.

4. Monitoring and Reviewing Risk

Effective risk management is not a one-time activity but a continuous process. It is essential to monitor and review the performance of risk management strategies regularly. This involves tracking the risk exposures of the portfolio, reassessing the identified risks, and evaluating the effectiveness of the mitigation techniques.

Regular *Performance Metrics*, such as Sharpe Ratio, Sortino Ratio, and Maximum Drawdown, are useful in assessing the risk-adjusted performance of a portfolio. Additionally, updating risk models in response to market conditions and incorporating feedback from stress tests can ensure that risk management remains robust and adaptive.

In sum, the fundamentals of risk management require a diligent and systematic approach involving the identification, quantification, mitigation, and continuous monitoring of risks. By embracing these principles, traders can enhance their ability to navigate the uncertainties of financial markets and achieve long-term success.

11.2 Types of Risks in Quantitative Trading

Understanding the types of risks inherent in quantitative trading is critical for developing robust strategies and resilient portfolios. This section delves into several key risk categories that quantitative traders must navigate to maintain stability and profitability.

Market Risk: Market risk, or systematic risk, arises from fluctuations in market prices due to economic, political, or other global events. These fluctuations can impact the entire market, making it impossible to fully avoid. The standard deviation and Value at Risk (VaR) are often used to quantify market risk. A common approach to mitigating market risk is through diversification and hedging techniques. For example, using derivatives such as options and futures can help hedge against adverse price movements in the underlying assets.

Credit Risk: Also known as counterparty risk, credit risk refers to the possibility that a counterparty will fail to fulfill its financial obligations. This risk is notably significant in the realm of over-the-counter (OTC) derivatives and fixed-income securities. Assessing creditworthiness through credit ratings and financial health analysis is essential. Modern quantitative models also incorporate credit default swap (CDS) spreads to estimate the default risk of counterparties.

Liquidity Risk: Liquidity risk emerges when a trader is unable to execute trades at desired prices due to insufficient market depth or trading volume. This can lead to significant slippage or the need to accept less favorable prices. Algorithms designed to detect and measure market liquidity, such as the Amihud illiquidity ratio or bid-ask spread metrics, are vital tools in assessing and managing this risk. Additionally, ensuring a balanced portfolio that avoids over-concentration in illiquid assets can help mitigate liquidity constraints.

Operational Risk: Operational risk encompasses losses stemming from internal failures such as coding errors, system outages, data breaches, and human mistakes. In the quantitative trading domain, reliance on technology and algorithms amplifies the importance of robust operational risk management. Implementing rigorous testing protocols, maintaining redundant systems, and enforcing strict compliance procedures are prudent measures to minimize this type of risk.

Model Risk: Model risk arises from inaccuracies or flaws in the mathematical models used for making trading decisions. Even small errors in model assumptions or parameter estimation can lead to substantial financial losses. Continuous model validation, back-testing, and incorporating stress testing are best practices to identify and address model risk. Additionally, ensemble modeling and diversification across different quantitative strategies can reduce dependence on any single model.

Execution Risk: Execution risk refers to the risk that a trade will not be executed as planned. This can be due to technical failures, latency, slippage, or price changes during the execution process. High-frequency trading systems and low-latency connections to exchanges are designed to mitigate such risks by ensuring timely and accurate trade execution. Traders might also use adaptive algorithms that adjust their strategies based on real-time market conditions to optimize execution.

Regulatory Risk: Regulatory risk involves the potential for financial loss due to changes in laws, regulations, or enforcement practices. Compliance with existing regulations and staying abreast of legislative developments is vital for risk management. Quantitative traders often need to incorporate regulatory changes into their models and operational procedures quickly to avoid penalties and ensure transparent, legal trading practices.

Event Risk: Event risk includes unforeseen occurrences such as geopolitical events, natural disasters, and sudden market discontinuities like flash crashes. These events can lead to extreme market reactions and significant financial impacts. Scenario analysis and stress testing can help anticipate potential outcomes of various events, enabling traders to develop contingency plans and responsive strategies.

Recognizing and addressing these diverse risk types is crucial for developing a holistic and effective risk management framework in quantitative trading. By systematically incorporating risk assessments and mitigation tactics into their strategies, traders can better navigate the complexities of the financial markets while striving to achieve consistent and sustainable returns.

11.3 Statistical Measures of Risk

In quantitative trading, understanding and measuring risk is paramount to developing robust trading strategies. Several statistical measures provide insights into different dimensions of risk, each offering a unique perspective on the potential downsides and volatility inherent in the market. Here, we delve into the most critical statistical measures, explaining their significance and application in quantitative trading.

One of the foundational measures of risk is the variance, denoted as σ^2. Variance measures the dispersion of returns from the mean, providing an indicator of volatility. Mathematically, variance for a set of returns $\{r_1, r_2, \ldots, r_n\}$ is calculated as:

$$\sigma^2 = \frac{1}{n-1} \sum_{i=1}^{n} (r_i - \mu)^2 \tag{11.3}$$

where μ is the mean return. A higher variance indicates greater volatility, signaling higher risk. Despite its simplicity, variance alone does not fully capture the risk scenario, especially since it treats positive and negative deviations symmetrically.

Building on variance, the standard deviation σ is another vital measure. It is simply the square root of the variance:

$$\sigma = \sqrt{\sigma^2} \tag{11.4}$$

Standard deviation is advantageous because it is expressed in the same units as the returns, making it more interpretable for traders.

While variance and standard deviation provide a general sense of volatility, they do not distinguish between upside and downside movements. Addressing this limitation, Value at Risk (VaR) is introduced. VaR estimates the maximum potential loss over a specific time frame with a given confidence level. For instance, a 95% VaR of $1 million means there is a 95% chance that losses will not exceed $1 million over the specified period. VaR can be calculated using historical simulation, variance-covariance method, or Monte Carlo simulation. For a normal distribution of returns, VaR at confidence level α is given by:

$$\text{VaR}_\alpha = \mu + \sigma \cdot \Phi^{-1}(\alpha) \tag{11.5}$$

where $\Phi^{-1}(\alpha)$ is the inverse of the cumulative distribution function of the normal distribution. Though widely used, VaR has been criticized for not capturing extreme events (tail risk) and its lack of sub-additivity.

To counter VaR's limitations, Conditional Value at Risk (CVaR), also known as Expected Shortfall (ES), is employed. CVaR measures the expected loss given that the loss has exceeded the VaR threshold. Mathematically, for a distribution F of returns, CVaR at confidence level α is:

$$\text{CVaR}_\alpha = \frac{1}{1-\alpha} \int_\alpha^1 \text{VaR}_p \, dp \qquad (11.6)$$

CVaR provides a more comprehensive risk measure since it considers the tail of the distribution, thus accounting for extreme losses.

Another important measure is the Sharpe Ratio, which assesses the risk-adjusted return of an investment. It is defined as the ratio of the excess return (return minus the risk-free rate) to the standard deviation of returns:

$$\text{Sharpe Ratio} = \frac{R_p - R_f}{\sigma_p} \qquad (11.7)$$

where R_p is the portfolio return, R_f is the risk-free rate, and σ_p is the standard deviation of portfolio returns. A higher Sharpe Ratio indicates better risk-adjusted performance.

Additional complexity and insight are provided by examining the skewness and kurtosis of the return distribution. Skewness measures the asymmetry of the return distribution. Positive skewness indicates a distribution with a long right tail, suggesting more frequent small losses with occasional large gains, while negative skewness indicates a long left tail, implying frequent small gains with occasional large losses. Mathematically, skewness is defined as:

$$\text{Skewness} = \frac{1}{n} \sum_{i=1}^{n} \left(\frac{r_i - \mu}{\sigma} \right)^3 \qquad (11.8)$$

Kurtosis, on the other hand, measures the "tailedness" of the distribution, specifically the propensity for extreme values. High kurtosis implies more outliers, indicating higher risk of extreme returns (either gains or losses). Kurtosis is calculated as:

$$\text{Kurtosis} = \frac{1}{n} \sum_{i=1}^{n} \left(\frac{r_i - \mu}{\sigma} \right)^4 \qquad (11.9)$$

where higher values of kurtosis indicate a higher likelihood of outlier events.

In summary, statistical measures of risk such as variance, standard deviation, VaR, CVaR, Sharpe Ratio, skewness, and kurtosis provide traders with diverse tools to quantify and manage risk. Each measure captures different aspects of risk, and their combined application leads to a more nuanced and comprehensive risk assessment, facilitating better decision-making in the volatile landscape of quantitative trading.

11.4   Risk Management Strategies and Tools

Effective risk management is the cornerstone of long-term success in quantitative trading. Traders and investors need to systematically identify, assess, and mitigate risks to protect their capital and ensure consistent performance. This section explores various strategies and tools that can be employed to manage risk effectively.

The primary objective of risk management strategies in quantitative trading is to minimize the potential for significant losses while optimizing the overall risk-return profile of the portfolio. This can be achieved through a combination of position sizing, hedging techniques, and the use of advanced financial instruments. Let's delve into these methodologies in detail.

One of the foundational strategies in risk management is position sizing. Determining the appropriate size of each trade relative to the total portfolio capital is crucial. The Kelly Criterion is a well-known formula used by traders to calculate the optimal size of a trade based on the expected return and the probability of success. Expressed mathematically, the Kelly Criterion is given by:

$$f^* = \frac{bp - q}{b}$$

where f^* is the fraction of the portfolio to risk, b is the net odds received on the wager (i.e., the profit-to-loss ratio), p is the probability of winning, and q is the probability of losing (which is $1 - p$).

Hedging is another powerful tool in the risk management arsenal. Traders use hedging strategies to offset potential losses in their primary positions by taking opposing positions in related assets. For example, a trader holding a long position in a stock might purchase put options on the same stock to protect against a decline in its price. The use of derivatives such as options, futures, and swaps allows traders to manage risk more dynamically and effectively.

Additionally, diversification remains a time-tested risk management tactic. By spreading investments across a variety of asset classes, sectors, and geographical regions, traders can reduce the impact of any one investment's poor performance on the overall portfolio. The principle of diversification is grounded in the fact that the risks associated with individual investments are not perfectly correlated, hence their combined risk can be lower than the risk of any single investment.

Quantitative traders also leverage sophisticated financial instruments and algorithms to manage risk. One such instrument is the Value-at-Risk (VaR) model, which estimates the potential loss in the value of a portfolio over a given time period, for a specified confidence interval. The VaR can be calculated using historical simulation, Monte Carlo simulation, or the parametric method, each having its own merits.

Consider the parametric VaR for a normally distributed portfolio's returns, computed as follows:

$$\text{VaR}_\alpha = \mu - z_\alpha \sigma$$

where μ is the mean of the portfolio returns, σ is the standard deviation of the portfolio returns, and z_α is the z-score corresponding to the confidence level α.

Beyond VaR, Conditional Value-at-Risk (CVaR) or Expected Shortfall (ES) provides a measure of the average loss that exceeds the VaR threshold. This metric is particularly useful in understanding the tail-risk in a portfolio, offering a more comprehensive view of potential extreme losses.

Risk management tools also include scenario analysis and stress testing. These techniques involve simulating the impact of extreme market events on a portfolio to evaluate its resilience. Scenario analysis considers specific hypothetical events, such as a sudden interest rate hike, geopolitical crisis, or financial market crash. Stress testing, on the other hand, applies extreme assumptions to various risk factors—such as drastic changes in volatility, liquidity, or asset prices—to assess the portfolio's behavior under severely adverse conditions.

Furthermore, regulatory requirements play a pivotal role in shaping the risk management practices of trading institutions. Regulations such as Basel III for banks and the Dodd-Frank Act for the financial industry impose strict guidelines and capital adequacy standards. Compliance with these regulations ensures that institutions maintain sufficient capital buffers and adopt robust risk management frameworks to safeguard against systemic risks.

The integration of these strategies and tools forms the backbone of a sound risk management framework. By combining rigorous quantitative methods with practical hedging and diversification techniques, traders can navigate the uncertainties of the financial markets with greater confidence and stability.

11.5   Portfolio Diversification

Diversification is a cornerstone of risk management in quantitative trading, often lauded as one of the most effective strategies for mitigating risk. At its core, diversification involves spreading investments across a variety of assets to reduce exposure to any single asset or risk. The fundamental principle is that a diversified portfolio will, on average, yield higher returns and pose a lower risk than any individual investment found within the portfolio. This section delves into the mechanics of portfolio diversification, illustrating its importance and offering practical strategies for implementation.

The principle of diversification derives from the observation that different assets often respond differently to economic events. By holding a range of assets, a portfolio can balance out the returns: when some assets perform poorly, others may perform well, thereby stabilizing overall performance. To understand diversification's mechanics, we first need to examine the concept of correlation.

The correlation coefficient, denoted as ρ, measures the linear relationship between two variables, in this case, asset returns. It ranges from -1 to 1, where:
$$\rho = \frac{\text{cov}(X, Y)}{\sigma_X \sigma_Y}$$

Here, $\text{cov}(X, Y)$ is the covariance of asset returns X and Y, and σ_X and σ_Y are the standard deviations of the returns of assets X and Y, respectively. A positive correlation implies that assets' returns tend to move in the same direction, whereas a negative correlation indicates they move in opposite directions.

Optimal diversification seeks assets with low, zero, or negative correlations, as these combinations reduce total portfolio risk. Mathematically, the risk (standard deviation) of a portfolio of two assets can be expressed as:

$$\sigma_p = \sqrt{w_1^2\sigma_1^2 + w_2^2\sigma_2^2 + 2w_1w_2\sigma_1\sigma_2\rho_{12}}$$

where:

- w_1 and w_2 represent the weights of the two assets in the portfolio,

- σ_1 and σ_2 are the standard deviations of the asset returns,

- ρ_{12} is the correlation coefficient between the returns of the two assets.

This formula illustrates how the portfolio's overall risk is a function of the individual assets' risks and their correlation. By carefully selecting assets with low or negative correlations, one can construct a portfolio that minimizes risk for a given level of expected return.

A practical approach to diversification involves various asset classes, including equities, fixed-income securities, commodities, and alternative investments like real estate or hedge funds. Each asset class responds differently to economic changes, interest rate fluctuations, and geopolitical events. Therefore, incorporating a mix of these assets can significantly enhance diversification.

For instance, consider equities and bonds. Historical data suggests that equities and bonds often exhibit low or negative correlations. Equities typically offer higher returns but come with higher volatility, whereas bonds provide more stable returns but lower yields. By holding both asset types, investors can achieve a more balanced risk-return profile.

Another strategy is geographic diversification, which involves investing in assets from different countries or regions. This approach can mitigate risks associated with economic downturns, political instability, or regulatory changes specific to a single country. However, it is essential to recognize the nuances of currency risk and cross-border tax implications when diversifying internationally.

Within the scope of quantitative trading, diversification also extends to different strategies and models.   By deploying various trading strategies—such as trend-following, mean reversion, and arbitrage—traders can diversify the sources of their returns.   Distinct strategies often perform differently under varying market conditions, thus balancing the portfolio's performance over time.

Moreover, a multidimensional diversification strategy that includes both asset and temporal diversification is equally crucial. Temporal diversification, or dollar-cost averaging, involves spreading out investments over time to reduce the impact of market volatility. By investing a fixed amount at regular intervals, traders can average out the costs and mitigate timing risks.

While diversification provides a robust framework for risk management, it is vital to continuously monitor and adjust the portfolio to reflect changing market conditions and correlations. The dynamic nature of financial markets means that correlations between assets can shift, necessitating ongoing reassessment and rebalancing to maintain optimal diversification.

Portfolio diversification, therefore, is not a one-time task but a continuous process. Traders and investors must remain vigilant, stay informed, and be prepared to adjust their portfolios to navigate the ever-changing market landscape effectively.   Through thoughtful diversification, investors can enhance their portfolios' stability and resilience, positioning themselves for long-term success.

11.6   Stress Testing and Scenario Analysis

Stress testing and scenario analysis are crucial techniques in risk management that help quantitative traders to anticipate and prepare for extreme market conditions. These methods are designed to evaluate how a trading portfolio might perform under adverse circumstances by simulating a range of extreme yet plausible scenarios. Addressing these scenarios allows traders to identify vulnerabilities in their portfolios and take preemptive measures to mitigate potential losses.

Stress testing involves creating hypothetical conditions that represent extreme market situations, such as sudden interest rate hikes, sharp declines in asset prices, or unexpected geopolitical events.   These stress scenarios are not necessarily derived from historical data but are intended to push the boundaries of current risk assumptions. The primary goal is to ensure that a portfolio can withstand significant volatility without incurring catastrophic losses.

Scenario analysis, on the other hand, typically involves constructing detailed narratives of specific events that could impact the financial markets. These narratives are based on historical occurrences or emerging risks and focus on how such events would influence various market variables and, consequently, the trading portfolio. Unlike stress testing, which emphasizes extreme conditions, scenario analysis encompasses a broader spectrum of potential market developments, including both extreme and moderate scenarios.

To illustrate the process, consider a trading portfolio with significant exposure to equities in emerging markets. A stress test might simulate a scenario where these markets experience a 30% drop in value within a short period, reflecting a crisis similar to the 1997 Asian Financial Crisis. Under this condition, the trader would analyze the effects on the portfolio, considering factors such as liquidity, correlation between assets, and potential margin calls.

In a scenario analysis, the trader might evaluate the impact of a trade war between major economies. This scenario could include a range of market responses, such as tariffs leading to decreased trade volumes, currency devaluations, and shifts in investor sentiment. The analysis would examine how these factors interact to influence the portfolio's performance over a more extended timeframe.

To perform effective stress testing and scenario analysis, quantitative traders often rely on advanced financial models and robust computational tools. These models need to incorporate various risk factors, including market risk, credit risk, liquidity risk, and operational risk. Historical data, while not always indicative of future performance, can provide valuable insights for constructing realistic stress scenarios.

One commonly used approach is the Value-at-Risk (VaR) model, which estimates the maximum expected loss over a specified period at a given confidence level. To strengthen the VaR model for stress testing, stress scenarios are introduced to capture potential tail risk events—those rare but severe outcomes that the standard VaR model might underestimate. By recalculating VaR under stressed conditions, traders can gain a better understanding of their exposure to extreme risks.

Another important tool is the Monte Carlo simulation, which generates a multitude of possible future paths for market variables based on their statistical properties. By inputting stress scenarios into the simulation, traders can observe how different aspects of the portfolio are affected under various conditions. This method provides a probabilistic distribution of potential outcomes, assisting traders in making informed decisions about risk management.

Implementing stress testing and scenario analysis also requires an ongoing assessment of emerging risks and market developments. For instance, regulatory changes, technological advancements, or economic shifts can introduce new types of risks that need to be incorporated into future stress and scenario tests. It is vital for traders to continuously update their models and assumptions to reflect the dynamic nature of financial markets.

The insights gained from these exercises can inform several risk management actions. Traders might realign their portfolios by reducing exposure to particularly vulnerable assets, increasing hedging activities, or diversifying into less correlated sectors. Additionally, they may optimize their capital allocation strategies to enhance resilience against anticipated market shocks.

Stress testing and scenario analysis not only aid in uncovering potential weaknesses in a portfolio but also contribute to regulatory compliance. Financial regulators often mandate that trading firms conduct regular stress tests to demonstrate their ability to manage and withstand financial disruptions. Compliance with these requirements is crucial for maintaining the firm's credibility and operational stability.

Ultimately, the value of stress testing and scenario analysis lies in their ability to prepare traders for uncertainty. By systematically examining potential adverse events and their impact on the portfolio, traders can develop robust risk management strategies that enhance their resilience to market volatility. This proactive approach not only safeguards assets but also builds confidence in the trader's ability to navigate an unpredictable financial environment.

11.7   Regulatory Requirements for Risk Management

Regulatory requirements are pivotal in ensuring that financial markets operate with integrity, fairness, and transparency. They serve as a backbone to risk management practices, reinforcing stability, and protecting both investors and institutions from unforeseen financial disruptions. Navigating the labyrinth of these regulations can be complex, but understanding their essence is crucial for constructing a robust risk management framework.

The landscape of financial regulation is shaped by various governing bodies across different jurisdictions. Key among these are the Securities and Exchange Commission (SEC) in the United States, the Financial Conduct Authority (FCA) in the United Kingdom, and the European Securities and Markets Authority (ESMA) in the European Union. These regulatory entities enact and enforce rules designed to prevent malpractice, ensuring that firms adhere to prudent risk management strategies.

One foundational aspect of regulatory requirements is the necessity for comprehensive disclosure. Firms are mandated to disclose their risk management policies, including methodologies for assessing market, credit, operational, and liquidity risks. Transparency in reporting not only fortifies market confidence but also aids regulators in monitoring systemic risk levels.

The Basel III framework, formulated by the Basel Committee on Banking Supervision, is an exemplary model of stringent risk management regulation. It sets out several critical measures:

$$\text{Capital Adequacy Ratios (CAR)} = \frac{\text{Tier 1 Capital} + \text{Tier 2 Capital}}{\text{Risk-Weighted Assets}}$$

Financial institutions must maintain a minimum CAR, ensuring they hold sufficient capital to withstand financial shocks. A cornerstone of Basel III is the leverage ratio, intended to curb excessive borrowing:

$$\text{Leverage Ratio} = \frac{\text{Tier 1 Capital}}{\text{Average Total Consolidated Assets}}$$

Additionally, the framework introduces liquidity requirements like the Liquidity Coverage Ratio (LCR) and Net Stable Funding Ratio (NSFR). These ratios ensure that institutions have adequate liquid assets to endure short-term liquidity stresses and to maintain stable funding over a one-year horizon, respectively.

In the world of quantitative trading, specific regulatory requirements around algorithmic trading are increasingly relevant. Regulations such as the European Union's Markets in Financial Instruments Directive II

(MiFID II) mandate that firms must have effective systems and risk controls in place for algorithmic trading activities. These controls include pre-trade risk limits to prevent erratic market behavior and mechanisms to halt trading should systems malfunction.

Furthermore, stress testing, mandated by regulators, is a critical tool for evaluating the resilience of trading strategies under hypothetical adverse conditions. The Dodd-Frank Wall Street Reform and Consumer Protection Act in the United States introduced rigorous stress testing requirements, compelling financial institutions to assess the impact of economic downturns on their portfolio.

Regulatory compliance extends to operational risk management, where firms must implement robust systems to mitigate risks associated with technological failures, human errors, and external events. Protocols such as the Sarbanes-Oxley Act (SOX) emphasize the importance of internal controls and audit requirements to prevent fraud and ensure accurate financial reporting.

Keeping abreast of regulatory changes is an ongoing requirement for financial institutions. Adapting to new regulations necessitates a dynamic and proactive approach to risk management. Integration of regulatory updates into financial models, continuous monitoring, and compliance auditing are practices that firms must embed into their operational fabric.

As we transition beyond foundational principles of risk regulation, it is evident that these requirements do more than just mandate compliance—they shape resilient, transparent, and equitable financial markets. This scaffolding of regulatory oversight provides the necessary framework within which risk management strategies can thrive, safeguarding not just individual firms, but the financial ecosystem at large.

Chapter 12

Future Directions in Market Microstructure

This chapter explores emerging trends and future directions in market microstructure, including the impact of artificial intelligence and machine learning. It examines the potential of blockchain and decentralized finance to revolutionize markets. The evolution of trading technologies and the associated regulatory challenges are discussed. The chapter also considers the growing importance of sustainable and ethical investing, and identifies promising areas for future research in market microstructure.

12.1 Emerging Trends in Market Microstructure

The landscape of market microstructure is continuously evolving, driven by technological advancements, shifting regulatory frameworks, and changing market participant behaviors. Understanding these emerging trends is crucial for investors and traders seeking to navigate the increasingly complex financial markets. This section delves into several key trends shaping market microstructure today, shedding light on how these developments are transforming the trading environment.

One of the most significant trends is the growing prevalence of high-frequency trading (HFT) and the use of sophisticated algorithms. HFT firms deploy advanced algorithms to execute a large number of trades at extremely high speeds, often leveraging milliseconds or microseconds to capture arbitrage opportunities. These activities have fundamentally altered the traditional market dynamics, increasing liquidity and tightening spreads, but also raising concerns about market stability and fairness. The debate over HFT's impact on markets continues, with researchers and regulators scrutinizing its role in market crashes and flash events.

Another notable trend is the increasing use of machine learning and artificial intelligence (AI) in trading strategies. These technologies have the potential to process vast amounts of data, identify complex patterns, and make predictive decisions at a scale and speed beyond human capabilities. For instance, natural language processing (NLP) techniques can analyze news articles, earnings reports, and social media posts to gauge market sentiment and predict price movements. The integration of AI and machine learning into trading not only promises enhanced performance but also poses new challenges, such as ensuring algorithmic transparency and mitigating the risk of overfitting.

The rise of alternative data sources is also reshaping the market microstructure landscape. Traditional financial data, while still vital, is being supplemented by non-conventional datasets derived from social media, satellite imagery, credit card transactions, and more. Traders and investors are increasingly leveraging these alternative data sources to gain unique insights and develop more informed trading strategies. The ability to harness and analyze such diverse datasets offers a competitive edge in predicting market trends and identifying investment opportunities.

Blockchain technology and decentralized finance (DeFi) represent another transformative trend. Blockchain's distributed ledger technology ensures transparency, security, and immutability, which are critical for trust in financial transactions. DeFi platforms open up new possibilities for trading, lending, and borrowing by eliminating intermediaries and enabling peer-to-peer financial services. These innovations have the potential to democratize financial markets, reduce transaction costs, and enhance market efficiency. However, they also bring about regulatory and security challenges that need to be addressed to ensure their sustainable integration into the broader financial system.

The adoption of smart contracts, facilitated by blockchain, is further revolutionizing trading and settlement processes. Smart contracts automatically execute predefined actions when certain conditions are met, streamlining operations and reducing the need for intermediaries. This automation can enhance efficiency, lower costs, and minimize human errors, but also requires robust coding and enforceable legal frameworks to manage the risks of malfunction and fraud.

The market microstructure is also being influenced by the increasing emphasis on sustainable and ethical investing. Investors are progressively integrating environmental, social, and governance (ESG) factors into their decision-making processes. This shift is driven by growing awareness of the long-term risks associated with unsustainable practices and the desire to align investments with personal values. As a result, there is rising demand for financial products that adhere to ESG principles, leading to the growth of green bonds, impact investing, and socially responsible mutual funds. This trend not only influences market behavior but also pressures companies to adopt more sustainable and ethical practices.

Technological advancements are also facilitating the development of more sophisticated trading platforms and tools. Innovations such as direct market access (DMA), dark pools, and consolidated tape systems enhance transparency and market access for different types of traders. DMA allows institutional investors to interact directly with order books, minimizing latency and reducing the impact of intermediaries. Dark pools provide venues for large trades to be executed away from the public market, reducing market impact and preserving anonymity. Consolidated tape systems aggregate trade data across multiple exchanges, providing a comprehensive view of market activity and improving price discovery.

Lastly, market microstructure is being shaped by global regulatory changes. Regulators are working to strike a balance between fostering innovation and ensuring market integrity. Policies aimed at increasing transparency, improving risk management, and protecting investors are being developed and implemented worldwide. For example, regulations like the EU's Markets in Financial Instruments Directive II (MiFID II) aim to enhance market transparency and investor protection while also placing stricter controls on high-frequency trading. Regulatory developments can have profound impacts on market microstructure, affecting everything from trading volumes to the types of strategies employed by market participants.

These emerging trends collectively underscore the dynamic nature of market microstructure. The interplay of technology, data, regulation, and investor behavior is driving the evolution of financial markets in unprecedented ways. Traders and investors must stay informed and adaptable, leveraging new tools and insights to navigate this ever-changing landscape effectively.

$$\text{Expected Return} = \sum_{i=1}^{n} w_i \cdot r_i$$

Trend	Impact on Market	Challenges
High-Frequency Trading	Increased liquidity, tighter spreads	Market stability, fairness concerns
Machine Learning and AI	Enhanced predictive capabilities	Algorithmic transparency, risk of overfitting
Alternative Data	Unique market insights	Data integration, reliability
Blockchain and DeFi	Reduced transaction costs, democratization	Regulatory issues, security risks
Sustainable Investing	Growth of ESG products	Measurement standards, impact verification
Regulatory Changes	Improved transparency and protection	Compliance costs, market adaptation

The illustration of these trends through the lens of their impacts and associated challenges provides a clearer understanding of how they are reshaping market microstructure. Staying abreast of these developments will be crucial for market participants aiming to thrive in this evolving environment.

12.2   Impact of Artificial Intelligence and Machine Learning

Artificial Intelligence (AI) and Machine Learning (ML) have revolutionized the landscape of financial markets, transforming the ways trades are executed, portfolios are managed, and strategies are developed. These technologies enable market participants to leverage algorithmic efficiencies and data-driven decisions, thereby enhancing performance and reducing the potential for human error.

The integration of AI and ML into trading practices allows for the processing of vast amounts of data at unparalleled speeds. Traditional analysis techniques often falter under the sheer volume and complexity of contemporary financial datasets. AI, with its advanced pattern recognition capabilities, can digest structured and unstructured data to uncover insights that are beyond human cognitive limits. Machine Learning models, in particular, are designed to identify and adapt to patterns within data, continuously improving their predictive power as more information becomes available.

Consider a common application such as predictive modeling for stock prices. Traditional models, such as linear regression, are often limited by their assumptions and simplifications. In contrast, ML models like neural networks, decision trees, or support vector machines can capture non-linearities and interactions within the data. For instance, a neural network might learn intricate relationships between numerous inputs—ranging from historical prices, trading volume, and macroeconomic indicators to sentiment derived from news articles and social media. This dynamic learning capability allows the model to evolve in response to new data, continuously refining its accuracy.

$$\text{Price}_{t+1} = f(\text{Price}_t, \text{Volume}_t, \text{Sentiment}_t, \text{Economic Indicators}_t, \ldots)$$

Furthermore, AI-driven algorithmic trading strategies have become prevalent. High-frequency trading (HFT) leverages AI to execute orders at microsecond intervals, seeking to capitalize on minute price discrepancies. These algorithms utilize sophisticated models and real-time data to make split-second decisions, performing thousands of trades in the time it would take a human trader to execute one. By reacting faster than humanly possible, these algorithms often achieve significant short-term gains, contributing to market liquidity and efficiency.

Simplified ML Model for Predictive Trading Signals

```
from sklearn.ensemble import RandomForestClassifier
import pandas as pd

# Load and preprocess data
data = pd.read_csv('market_data.csv')
features = data[['price', 'volume', 'sentiment', 'economic_indicators']].values
labels = data['future_price_movement'].values

# Initialize and train model
model = RandomForestClassifier(n_estimators=100)
model.fit(features, labels)

# Predict future price movement
```

```
prediction = model.predict(new_data)
```

The predictive prowess and capacity for risk management provided by AI and ML also enhance portfolio management. Advanced algorithms can optimize asset allocation by not only considering expected returns and volatility but also dynamically adjusting for changing market conditions. Techniques like reinforcement learning can be employed where the algorithm learns to optimize the returns by adjusting the weights of assets in the portfolio based on historical performance and predicted future states.

In the domain of risk management, AI and ML excel at identifying potential risks and mitigating them before they lead to significant losses. Models can forecast potential market downturns by analyzing historical trends and predicting the impact of new information. Moreover, anomaly detection algorithms can flag irregular trading patterns or financial fraud, providing a robust safeguard against market manipulations.

$$\text{Portfolio Return} = \sum_{i=1}^{n} w_i \cdot r_i \quad \text{where} \quad w_i = \text{weight of asset } i, \ r_i = \text{return of asset } i$$

Despite these advancements, it is crucial to acknowledge potential challenges and limitations. AI models are often regarded as "black boxes," making it difficult to interpret the exact reasoning behind their predictions. This opacity can be problematic, especially in high-stakes environments where understanding the model's decision-making process is critical. Overreliance on AI could also lead to complacency, where traders become excessively dependent on automated systems, potentially overlooking market nuances that a human would catch. Furthermore, the models are only as good as the data they are trained on. Poor-quality or biased data can lead to flawed models and suboptimal trading strategies.

With the rapid evolution of AI and ML technologies, regulatory frameworks need to adapt to ensure fair and transparent markets. Regulators must balance the benefits of technological adoption with the necessity of safeguarding market integrity and protecting investors. Efforts to promote transparency in AI-driven trading practices are essential, as is fostering collaboration between technologists, economists, and policymakers.

AI and ML are not just transformative tools but also represent the future trajectory of market microstructure research. As these technologies

196

continue to mature, their integration into financial markets will likely produce more sophisticated and resilient trading ecosystems. The perpetual advancement of AI, coupled with rigorous research and ethical considerations, will shape the next frontier of financial trading and investing.

This progression hinging on AI and ML heralds an era where markets are more efficient, intelligent, and adaptive. Market participants equipped with cutting-edge tools stand to gain unprecedented insights and opportunities, continually pushing the boundaries of what's possible in trading and investment strategies.

12.3 Blockchain and Decentralized Finance

The landscape of financial markets is undergoing a transformation, significantly influenced by the advent of blockchain technology and decentralized finance (DeFi). These innovations hold the potential to revolutionize trading infrastructure by enhancing transparency, security, and efficiency. This section delves into the foundational aspects of blockchain and DeFi, exploring their implications for market microstructure.

The blockchain is a decentralized ledger technology (DLT) that underpins cryptocurrencies like Bitcoin and Ethereum. It records transactions across a network of computers, ensuring that the history of a digital asset is immutable and transparent. DeFi extends the capabilities of blockchain by facilitating financial services through decentralized applications (dApps) on public blockchains. This system aims to recreate and improve upon traditional financial systems by eliminating intermediaries and introducing programmable, automated financial instruments.

A key advantage of blockchain technology is its ability to provide a single, immutable source of truth. Each block in the chain contains a list of transactions, and once validated and added to the ledger, it cannot be altered without consensus from the network. This integrity is maintained using cryptographic hashing and a consensus algorithm, commonly Proof of Work (PoW) or Proof of Stake (PoS). The concept of smart contracts, integral to Ethereum's blockchain, further enhances this system. Smart contracts are self-executing contracts where the terms of the agreement are directly written into code, automating and ensuring the reliable execution of transactions.

$$H(n) = H_1(H_0 + T(n))$$

Here, $H(n)$ represents the hash of the current block, H_0 is the hash of the previous block, and $T(n)$ accounts for the information in the transactions within the current block. This chaining mechanism secures the blockchain against tampering and fraud.

In the realm of decentralized finance, blockchain technology facilitates various financial services without traditional financial intermediaries. Some prominent DeFi applications include lending and borrowing platforms, decentralized exchanges (DEXs), stablecoins, and yield farming. DeFi platforms use automated market makers (AMMs) instead of traditional order books, which provide liquidity through pooled assets and determine prices using smart contract algorithms.

$$AMM : P_x \cdot P_y = k$$

In an Automated Market Maker, P_x and P_y are the prices of the assets in the pool, and k is a constant. The product of the asset prices remains constant, ensuring liquidity and facilitating price discovery in decentralized exchanges.

One significant impact of DeFi on market microstructure is the democratization of financial services. By leveraging blockchain technology, DeFi platforms can offer services to anyone with an internet connection, bypassing geographic and regulatory barriers. This inclusion promotes higher market participation, potentially increasing market liquidity and resiliency.

Moreover, the transparency of blockchain and DeFi protocols enhances trust among market participants. All transactions and smart contract codes are publicly accessible, allowing for real-time audit and verification. This openness can reduce information asymmetry, a common issue in traditional finance, where counterparties often operate with varying levels of knowledge and access to information.

The integration of blockchain and DeFi in trading infrastructure also raises significant regulatory challenges. Traditional financial markets are heavily regulated to ensure stability, protect investors, and maintain fair trading practices. However, the decentralized and global nature of blockchain technology complicates regulatory oversight. Jurisdictions worldwide are striving to develop frameworks that can accommodate these innovations while mitigating risks such as money laundering, fraud, and cyber threats.

Innovative solutions, such as decentralized identity (DID) and self-sovereign identity (SSI), are being explored to align DeFi practices with regulatory requirements. These solutions aim to provide verifiable, privacy-preserving identification methods that can satisfy Know Your Customer (KYC) and Anti-Money Laundering (AML) norms without compromising user privacy.

Given the rapid development in blockchain and DeFi, continuous research is crucial to understand their evolving dynamics and potential implications for market microstructure fully. Areas of interest include scalability solutions, interoperability between different blockchain networks, and the development of standardized regulatory frameworks that can address peculiarities of decentralized systems.

Blockchain and DeFi represent a significant shift in how financial markets operate. Their capacity to deliver decentralized, transparent, and efficient trading mechanisms can potentially redefine market microstructure. As these technologies mature, their ability to integrate with traditional financial systems and comply with regulatory standards will likely dictate their long-term impact and adoption.

This exploration of blockchain and decentralized finance underscores their transformative potential in market microstructure. These technologies offer promising solutions to longstanding inefficiencies and inequalities within traditional financial systems, paving the way for a more inclusive and transparent financial future.

12.4 Evolution of Trading Technologies

The landscape of trading technologies has undergone a monumental transformation over the past few decades, reshaping the way market participants interact and execute trades. This section delves into the key innovations and shifts that have characterized this evolution, highlighting their implications for traders, investors, and the broader financial ecosystem.

In the early days, trading was predominantly conducted via open outcry systems on trading floors, such as the New York Stock Exchange (NYSE). Traders would physically congregate to shout buy and sell orders, a process that was not only labor-intensive but also prone to human error and delays. The first significant leap towards modern trading technologies came with the advent of electronic trading platforms in the 1970s. These platforms allowed for the electronic matching of buy and sell orders, thereby increasing efficiency and reducing the reliance on human operators.

One of the early milestones in electronic trading was the introduction of the NASDAQ in 1971. As the first electronic stock market, NASDAQ provided a robust framework for the automated execution of trades, which, in turn, democratized access to markets by allowing a broader range of participants to engage in trading activities. This shift was further propelled by the development of the Securities Automated Quotations (SEQ) system, which enabled real-time tracking of stock prices.

The next major phase in the evolution of trading technologies was the rise of algorithmic trading in the late 1990s and early 2000s. Algorithmic trading involves the use of computer algorithms to execute trades at speeds and frequencies impossible for human traders. These algorithms can be designed to follow specific strategies, such as arbitrage, trend following, or market making. The proliferation of high-frequency trading (HFT) is a direct consequence of advancements in algorithmic trading. HFT leverages state-of-the-art technology to execute large volumes of orders at extremely high speeds, often completing transactions within microseconds. This development has sparked debates regarding market fairness and stability due to the advantages offered to traders with superior technological infrastructure.

As computing power and data analytics have continued to advance, the integration of artificial intelligence (AI) and machine learning (ML) into trading strategies has become increasingly prevalent. These technologies enable the analysis of vast datasets to identify patterns and anomalies that might not be apparent through traditional analytical methods. AI and ML models can adapt to changing market conditions and continuously optimize trading strategies, offering a significant edge to market participants who can harness these capabilities effectively.

Blockchain technology and decentralized finance (DeFi) represent another frontier in the evolution of trading technologies. Blockchain's ability to provide a secure, transparent, and immutable ledger has profound implications for the trading world. Decentralized exchanges (DEXs), built on blockchain platforms, facilitate peer-to-peer trading without the need for traditional intermediaries. This has the potential to reduce costs, increase trading speed, and enhance market accessibility. Additionally, the rise of smart contracts enables automated and trustless trading operations, further innovating the landscape of trading technologies.

The regulatory environment surrounding trading technologies has also needed to evolve in response to these technological advancements. Regulatory bodies have introduced various measures to ensure market integrity and protect investors. For example, after the "Flash Crash" of 2010, the U.S. Securities and Exchange Commission (SEC) implemented circuit breakers and other safeguards to stabilize the market. Continuous monitoring and adaptation of regulations are essential as technologies evolve to mitigate risks and preserve a level playing field.

The convergence of these advanced trading technologies has significantly impacted market microstructure. Trading costs have generally decreased, market liquidity has improved, and the speed of trade executions has reached unprecedented levels. However, it also poses challenges, such as heightened competition and the need for constant upgrades to technological infrastructure to maintain a competitive edge.

Looking ahead, the continued evolution of trading technologies will likely be influenced by ongoing advancements in AI, quantum computing, and blockchain. The integration of these technologies could lead to even greater market efficiencies and new forms of financial instruments. As such, staying informed about technological trends and developments is crucial for all market participants to adapt and thrive in an increasingly complex and dynamic trading environment.

In essence, the evolution of trading technologies is a testament to the continuous innovation and ingenuity within financial markets. By understanding this evolution, traders and investors can better navigate the current landscape and anticipate future changes that may shape the world of trading.

12.5 Regulatory Challenges and Future Directions

As the landscape of financial markets continues to evolve, the regulatory environment must adapt to keep pace with rapid technological advancements. Regulatory challenges in market microstructure are multifaceted, encompassing areas such as algorithmic trading, market transparency, systemic risk, and the impact of emerging technologies like blockchain and artificial intelligence.

A core aspect of modern regulatory frameworks is ensuring that algorithmic trading is conducted in a fair and transparent manner. Algo-rithmic trading, while providing significant benefits in terms of liquidity and efficiency, also poses risks such as market manipulation and flash crashes. Regulators are increasingly focused on developing guidelines that demand robust risk management practices from trading firms. This includes implementing sophisticated surveillance systems to detect ir-regular trading patterns and holding firms accountable for their algorith-mic strategies.

Another critical area of concern is market transparency. As trading venues become more complex with the proliferation of dark pools and alternative trading systems, ensuring that all market participants have equitable access to information becomes more challenging. Regula-tory bodies are working on policies that require greater disclosure of trading activities and order routing practices. Enhanced transparency rules aim to balance the need for anonymity in trading large blocks of securities with the requirement for a fair and orderly market.

Systemic risk is an additional regulatory focus, particularly following the global financial crisis of 2008. The interconnectedness of finan-cial institutions and markets warrants rigorous oversight to prevent cas-cading failures. Tools such as stress testing and capital adequacy re-quirements serve as preventive measures against systemic disruptions. Moreover, the introduction of centralized clearing for over-the-counter derivatives is a regulatory response aimed at reducing counterparty risk.

The advent of blockchain technology and decentralized finance intro-duces both opportunities and regulatory complexities. Blockchain of-fers the promise of enhanced transparency, reduced settlement times, and lower costs. However, it also brings up issues related to security, fraud prevention, and legal recognition of smart contracts. Regulatory approaches to blockchain are still in their infancy, with ongoing debates on how to integrate this technology within existing legal frameworks while mitigating associated risks.

Artificial intelligence (AI) and machine learning (ML) are reshaping financial markets with predictive analytics and automated decision-making processes. These technologies can enhance market efficiency but also pose risks when algorithms operate without sufficient trans-parency or oversight. Regulatory bodies are contemplating frameworks that ensure AI and ML systems are auditable, accountable, and de-signed with safeguards to prevent unintended consequences.

Looking towards the future, regulatory directions may increasingly focus on the following areas:

- **Dynamic Regulation:** Traditional regulatory approaches may be too rigid for the fast-evolving financial landscape. Dynamic regulation, which leverages real-time data and AI for continuous oversight, could become a cornerstone of future regulatory strategies. This would allow regulators to detect and respond to market anomalies more swiftly.

- **Global Coordination:** Financial markets are inherently global, and regulatory discrepancies between jurisdictions can lead to regulatory arbitrage. Greater international cooperation and harmonization of regulations will be essential in addressing cross-border financial activities and ensuring a coherent global financial system.

- **Ethical and Sustainable Investing:** With an increasing emphasis on environmental, social, and governance (ESG) factors, regulations will likely evolve to promote sustainable and ethical investing. This includes mandating disclosures related to ESG performance and integrating these considerations into risk assessment frameworks.

- **Consumer Protection:** As financial products become more complex, there is a growing need to ensure that investors, particularly retail investors, are adequately protected. This involves enhancing disclosure requirements, simplifying financial product structures, and ensuring that advisory processes are transparent and free from conflicts of interest.

In conclusion, the regulatory landscape of market microstructure must continuously adapt to technological innovations and emerging market practices. By developing forward-thinking, flexible, and globally coordinated regulatory approaches, authorities can foster markets that are both efficient and resilient, while protecting the interests of all market participants.

12.6   Sustainable and Ethical Investing

In recent years, there has been a notable shift in investor preferences towards sustainable and ethical investing. This trend is grounded in the growing awareness of the environmental and social impact of investment activities. Investors are increasingly motivated not only by financial returns but also by a desire to contribute positively to society and the planet. This section delves deeply into the principles, strategies, and implications of sustainable and ethical investing, providing a comprehensive understanding that aligns with the overall progression of market microstructure.

Sustainable investing refers to the practice of incorporating environmental, social, and governance (ESG) factors into investment decisions. This approach aims to generate long-term competitive financial returns while simultaneously fostering positive societal impact. Ethical investing, on the other hand, is guided by the ethical values and principles of the investor, often emphasizing the avoidance of investments in industries or practices deemed harmful or unethical, such as tobacco, firearms, and fossil fuels.

The integration of ESG factors into financial analysis allows investors to identify opportunities and risks that may not be apparent through traditional financial metrics. For example, a company's environmental practices can significantly affect its long-term viability and regulatory compliance, while its governance structures can influence operational efficiency and ethical conduct.

To implement sustainable and ethical investing strategies, investors can employ several key approaches:

- 1. **Exclusionary Screening:** This strategy involves excluding companies or sectors that do not meet certain ethical or sustainability criteria. Commonly excluded industries include tobacco, weapons, gambling, and fossil fuels. Exclusionary screening is straightforward to apply and aligns closely with investors' ethical standards.

  $$\text{Exclusionary Screening} = \{x \in \text{Companies} \mid \text{sectors}(x) \notin \text{Excluded Sectors}\}$$

- 2. **Positive Screening:** Positive screening focuses on identifying and investing in companies that demonstrate strong ESG performance. This approach rewards companies that are leaders in sustainability practices, such as renewable energy initiatives, fair labor practices, and robust governance policies. It involves detailed ESG performance evaluation using both quantitative and qualitative metrics.

- 3. **Thematic Investing:** Thematic investing targets specific themes or sectors expected to benefit from long-term sustainabil-

204

ity trends, such as clean energy, water conservation, or social impact enterprises. By concentrating on these themes, investors align their portfolios with broader macroeconomic and environmental shifts anticipated over the coming decades.

- 4. **Engagement and Shareholder Advocacy:** Shareholders actively engage with companies to influence their policies and practices towards more sustainable outcomes. This may involve dialogue with corporate management, filing shareholder resolutions, and voting on ESG issues. Such engagement can lead to meaningful change within companies and contribute to better overall ESG performance.

$$\text{Engagement Score} = \sum_{i=1}^{N} \text{Impact}_i \times \text{Probability of Success}_i$$

- 5. **Impact Investing:** Impact investing seeks to generate measurable social or environmental impacts alongside financial returns. This strategy focuses on sectors like renewable energy, affordable housing, microfinance, and education. Impact investments are typically evaluated using both traditional financial performance metrics and specific impact metrics such as carbon footprint reduction or number of beneficiaries.

The growing importance of sustainable and ethical investing is reflected in significant changes within market microstructure. The increased demand for ESG-compliant assets has led to the development of new financial products, such as green bonds, ESG-focused exchange-traded funds (ETFs), and sustainability-linked loans. These innovations provide investors with more tools to align their portfolios with their values.

Furthermore, regulatory frameworks and industry standards are evolving to support sustainable investing. Agencies like the United Nations Principles for Responsible Investment (UNPRI) and the Task Force on Climate-related Financial Disclosures (TCFD) have established guidelines to promote transparency and accountability in ESG reporting. Regulators in various jurisdictions are also introducing policies to encourage or mandate ESG disclosure, enhancing the availability of pertinent data for investors.

As sustainable and ethical investing continues to gain traction, it is crucial for investors to remain vigilant about "greenwashing"—where companies or funds exaggerate or falsely represent the extent of their ESG initiatives. Conducting thorough due diligence and utilizing third-party ESG ratings can help mitigate this risk.

Reflecting on the future, sustainable and ethical investing is poised to play an ever more pivotal role in shaping financial markets. By integrating ESG criteria into investment strategies, investors can not only achieve substantial financial returns but also contribute to a more sustainable and equitable global economy. As these practices continue to evolve, regular research and adaptation will be essential in maintaining their effectiveness and relevance in the ever-changing landscape of market microstructure.

12.7 Future Research Areas in Market Microstructure

Future research in market microstructure aims to address the rapid evolution of financial markets driven by technological innovation and dynamic regulatory landscapes. This section highlights several promising areas that warrant further investigation to deepen our understanding of market mechanics, improve trading efficiency, and ensure market integrity.

One of the most compelling areas for future research is the integration of artificial intelligence and machine learning in trading strategies. While significant strides have been made in algorithmic trading, the application of advanced AI techniques such as deep learning and reinforcement learning to optimize trading algorithms remains relatively nascent. Research could explore how these advanced models can enhance predictive accuracy, adapt to changing market conditions, and manage risks more effectively. Moreover, studies could investigate the ethical implications and potential biases embedded within AI-driven trading systems, ensuring these technologies promote fair and transparent markets.

Blockchain technology and decentralized finance (DeFi) present another rich vein for exploration. Researchers could delve into the mechanics of decentralized exchanges (DEXs) and automated market makers (AMMs), examining their impact on liquidity, pricing efficiency, and market stability. Additionally, there is a need to analyze the regulatory challenges posed by these innovations and develop frameworks that balance innovation with investor protection. Future studies might also consider the effects of tokenization of assets on traditional market structures and the implications for asset liquidity and price discovery.

The evolution of trading technologies continues to offer vast research potential, particularly in the areas of low-latency trading and high-frequency trading (HFT). Researchers could investigate the trade-offs between speed and market fairness, examining how latency arbitrage and ultra-fast trading strategies influence market dynamics. As trading platforms become more sophisticated, there is also an opportunity to explore the enhancement of surveillance mechanisms using advanced analytics to detect market manipulation and insider trading more effectively.

Regulatory challenges and future directions remain a critical area of focus for market microstructure research. The dynamic interplay between regulation and market innovation necessitates continuous study to ensure regulatory frameworks keep pace with technological advances. Future research might concentrate on the effectiveness of current regulations in mitigating systemic risks and protecting investors, while also encouraging financial innovation. Comparative studies across different jurisdictions could provide insights into best practices and the implications of regulatory divergence on global markets.

Sustainable and ethical investing is increasingly becoming a cornerstone of modern financial markets. Future research could investigate how market microstructure principles can be applied to promote sustainability and social responsibility in trading practices. Studies might analyze the impact of Environmental, Social, and Governance (ESG) criteria on market liquidity, volatility, and returns. Additionally, there is a growing need to develop robust metrics and benchmarks for evaluating the effectiveness of ESG investments, ensuring that they contribute meaningfully to societal goals.

Lastly, interdisciplinary research that bridges market microstructure with fields such as behavioral finance, data science, and network theory could yield innovative perspectives. Understanding the behavior of market participants through a behavioral lens could uncover anomalies and inefficiencies that traditional models overlook. Applying network theory could reveal the intricate relationships and interdependencies within financial markets, offering insights into systemic risks and the propagation of shocks.

The future of market microstructure research is poised to be as dynamic as the markets themselves. By exploring these areas with rigor and creativity, researchers can contribute to more efficient, fair, and resilient financial markets.

www.ingramcontent.com/pod-product-compliance
Lightning Source LLC
Chambersburg PA
CBHW061249220326
41599CB00028B/5590